CHOOSING WISELY: A GUIDE TO PREMARITAL COUNSELLING

By
Pastor Innocent C. Ugo

Published by
Faunteewrites

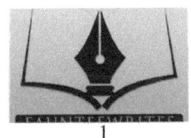

CHOOSING WISELY: A GUIDE TO PREMARITAL COUNSELLING

By
Pastor Innocent C. Ugo

Copyright © Pastor Innocent C. Ugo 2025.

Chika I. Ugo has asserted her right under the Copyright, Designs, and Patents Act 1988 to be identified as the author of this work.

This book is sold subject to the condition that it shall not, by way of trade or otherwise, be lent, resold, hired out, or otherwise circulated without the publisher's prior consent in any form of binding or cover other than that in which it is published and without a similar condition, including this condition, being imposed on the subsequent buyer.

Published by Faunteewrites Limited, Royal Arsenal Gatehouse, London, SE18 6AR.

Addresses for Faunteewrites limited can be found at: www.fauntee.co.uk

A CIP catalogue record for this book is available from the British Library

ISBN:

978-1-913103-15-6 - Paperback

978-1-913103-16-3 - Epub

Without limiting the rights under copyrights reserved above, no part of this publication may be reproduced, stored in or introduced into a retrieval system, or transmitted, in any way or form, or by means (electronic or mechanical, photocopying, recording, or otherwise), without the prior written permission of both the copyright owner and the publisher.

TABLE OF CONTENTS

Background and Introduction..7

Aims and Objectives..8

CHAPTER 1: The Meaning of Marriage..10

CHAPTER 2: Difference Between a Partner and a Spouse..18

CHAPTER 3. Causes of Divorce and Single Motherhood 21

CHAPTER 4: Biblical Principles Defining a Successful Marriage...............................27

CHAPTER 5: Differences from Secular Views on Marriage......................................31

CHAPTER 6: Christian teachings on love and commitment 33

CHAPTER 7: Best Ways to Foster Unity in Marriages Supported by Bible Verses.............37

CHAPTER 8: 12 Essential Things to Help Couples Grow Together in Christ....................48

CHAPTER 9: Factors Contributing to Marital Failure...51

CHAPTER 10: Understanding Divorce in the Context of Biblical Teachings....................77

CHAPTER 11: The Importance of Choosing the Right Partner...................................79

Chapter 12: Spiritual Compatibility...81

Chapter 13: Character and Integrity..83

Chapter 14: Purpose and Vision Alignment...89

Chapter 15: Communication and Understanding...91

Chapter 16: Emotional Maturity and Stability...94

Chapter 17: Financial Responsibility 97

Chapter 18: Family Background and Values... 100

Chapter 19: Mutual Respect and Love.. 103

Chapter 20: Conflict Resolution Skills... 107

CHAPTER 21 :Common Red Flags to Avoid 109

(1 Corinthians 15:33).. 109

CHAPTER 22: Counselling Questions for Each Session in the Premarital 111

Reflective Note from the Author... 141

References 142

BACKGROUND AND INTRODUCTION

In a world where relationships are often tested by external pressures and internal conflicts, the importance of premarital counselling cannot be overstated. Choosing Wisely: A Guide to Premarital Counselling by Pastor Innocent C. Ugo emerges as a beacon of hope for both unmarried and married individuals seeking to navigate the complexities of love, commitment, and partnership. This book is not merely a guide; it is a comprehensive resource that explores the essential elements of building a strong foundation for lasting relationships.

Pastor Innocent C. Ugo's years of experience in pastoral care and relationship counselling offer readers invaluable insights drawn from both scripture and practical wisdom. The book addresses common challenges faced by couples today, including communication barriers, financial stressors, family dynamics, and differing life goals. The aim of Choosing Wisely is to equip readers with the necessary tools to cultivate healthy relationships that can withstand the test of time.

The journey towards a successful marriage begins long before the wedding day. This book highlights the importance of intentional preparation, encouraging couples to explore their values, expectations, and aspirations together. Through thought-provoking questions, real-life examples, and actionable advice, Pastor Ugo guides readers in making informed decisions about their relationships.

AIMS AND OBJECTIVES

The primary aim of Choosing Wisely: A Guide to Premarital Counselling is to empower individuals, whether single or married, to make thoughtful choices regarding their romantic relationships. The objectives outlined in this book are designed to facilitate personal growth and relational understanding.

1. **Enhance Communication Skills:** A key objective is to help couples develop effective communication strategies that promote openness and understanding. Learning how to express feelings constructively and listen actively allows partners to build trust and intimacy.

2. **Identify Core Values:** This book encourages readers to reflect on their core values and beliefs about love, family, and commitment. Understanding these foundational aspects will enable couples to align their goals and expectations more closely.

3. **Address Conflict Resolution:** Conflicts are inevitable in any relationship; thus, this guide provides practical techniques for resolving disagreements amicably. Couples will learn how to approach conflicts with empathy rather than hostility.

4. **Prepare for Life Transitions:** Marriage often comes with significant life changes, be it financial responsibilities or parenting challenges. This book prepares couples for these transitions by discussing potential scenarios they may face together.

5. **Foster Spiritual Growth:** recognising that many individuals seek spiritual guidance in their relationships, Pastor Ugo integrates biblical principles throughout the text. Readers will find encouragement in faith-based practices that strengthen their bond.

6. **Promote Lifelong Learning:** Lastly, Choosing Wisely instills a mindset of

continuous growth within relationships. Couples are encouraged to view their journey as an evolving process where learning from experiences leads to deeper connections.

Through its relatable content and practical exercises, Choosing Wisely effectively addresses these aims, serving as an essential companion for those seeking to enrich their understanding of premarital counselling and ultimately fostering healthier relationships filled with love and respect.

CHAPTER 1: THE MEANING OF MARRIAGE

Marriage is a legally and socially recognised union between individuals that establishes rights and obligations between them, as well as between them and their children and in-laws. It is often seen as a foundational institution in many cultures, serving various purposes, including emotional support, economic stability, and the raising of children. In religious contexts, marriage can also be viewed as a sacred covenant.

In Christianity, marriage is often defined as a covenant relationship ordained by God. This perspective highlights the spiritual significance of the union, where both partners commit to love and support each other in accordance with biblical principles. The Bible describes marriage in Genesis 2:24 (NIV): "That is why a man leaves his father and mother and is united to his wife, and they become one flesh." This verse highlights the idea of unity and commitment inherent in the marital relationship.

Differences Between Godly and Ungodly Marriages

Understanding Godly Marriage

A godly marriage refers to a union between two individuals that is founded on spiritual principles and values as outlined in religious texts, particularly the Bible. It emphasises the importance of faith, love, mutual respect, and commitment to God's teachings. A Godly marriage seeks to reflect the relationship between Christ and the Church, promoting a partnership that honours God.

Key Principles of a Godly Marriage

Covenant Relationship: Unlike a contract, which can be broken, a covenant is a sacred agreement. In a Godly marriage, both partners commit to each other for life, mirroring God's unwavering commitment to humanity.

Mutual Submission: Ephesians 5:21 states, "Submit to one another out of reverence for Christ." This principle encourages spouses to prioritise each other's needs and desires.

Love and Respect: Ephesians 5:33 emphasises that husbands should love their wives as they love themselves, and wives should respect their husbands. This mutual affection fosters a nurturing environment.

Faith as Foundation: A strong spiritual foundation is crucial. Couples are encouraged to pray together, study scripture, and grow in their faith collectively.

Forgiveness and Grace: No marriage is without challenges; thus, practising forgiveness is essential. Colossians 3:13 advises believers to forgive as the Lord forgave them.

Biblical Examples of Godly Marriages

Adam and Eve (Genesis 2:24): Their union symbolises the divine design for marriage – two becoming one flesh.

Ruth and Boaz (Book of Ruth): Their story illustrates loyalty, kindness, and God's providence in relationships.

Mary and Joseph (Matthew 1): They exemplified trust in God's plan despite societal challenges.

Inspirational Quotes and Slogans

"A successful marriage requires falling in love many times, always with the same person." – Mignon McLaughlin

"Marriage is not just about finding someone you can live with; it's about finding someone you can't live without."

"Together we can face any challenges as deep as the ocean and as high as the sky."

Bible Verses for Guidance

1 Corinthians 13:4-7: "Love is patient, love is kind. It does not envy, it does not boast, it is not proud... It always protects, always trusts, always hopes, always perseveres."

Proverbs 18:22: "He who finds a wife finds what is good and receives favour from the Lord."

Ecclesiastes 4:9-12: "Two are better than one because they have a good return for their labour..."

Advice for Those Entering Marriage

- Prioritise your relationship with God individually and together.
- Communicate openly about expectations and dreams.
- Establish shared goals that align with your faith.
- Seek counsel from experienced couples or mentors within your faith community.
- Regularly engage in activities that strengthen your bond – prayer meetings or Bible studies together can be beneficial.

A godly marriage is characterised by adherence to biblical principles and teachings with the following key features:

Covenantal Commitment: A godly marriage is viewed as a lifelong commitment before God. Malachi 2:14 (NIV) states, "The Lord is acting as the witness between you and the wife of your youth because you have broken faith with her." This indicates that God holds couples accountable for their vows.

Mutual Respect and Love: Ephesians 5:25 (NIV) instructs husbands to love their wives just as Christ loved the church. This sacrificial love fosters an environment of respect and care.

Spiritual Growth: Couples are encouraged to grow together spiritually through prayer, worship, and studying scripture together (Ecclesiastes 4:12).

Purposeful Partnership: A godly marriage seeks to fulfil God's purpose for both individuals within the context of their union (Genesis 1:28).

Non-Godly Marriage: Understanding Non-Godly Marriage

Non-Godly Marriage refers to a union that does not align with the principles and teachings found in religious texts, particularly the Bible. This concept often encompasses marriages that lack spiritual foundation, commitment to faith-based values, or adherence to Christian guidelines regarding relationships and family life.

Characteristics of Non-Godly Marriages

1. **Lack of Spiritual Foundation:** These marriages may not involve shared beliefs or practices related to faith. Partners might prioritise secular values over spiritual ones.
2. **Absence of Commitment to Biblical Principles:** Non-Godly marriages may disregard biblical teachings about love, respect, fidelity, and the sanctity of marriage.
3. **Focus on Self-Interest:** In such unions, individuals might prioritise personal desires or societal expectations rather than mutual growth and support rooted in faith.
4. **Conflict with Religious Teachings:** These marriages may involve behaviours or lifestyles that contradict religious doctrines, such as infidelity or cohabitation before marriage without commitment.

Examples of Non-Godly Marriages

1. **Cohabitation Without Marriage:** Couples living together without the commitment of marriage often do not adhere to biblical teachings about sexual purity and the sanctity of marriage.
2. **Marriages Based on Convenience:** Unions formed for financial stability or social status rather than love and mutual respect can be seen as non-Godly.
3. **Interfaith Marriages Without Respect for Beliefs:** When partners from different faiths marry but do not respect each other's beliefs or fail to find common ground in their spiritual lives.

Biblical Verses Related to Marriage

1. **Ephesians 5:31-33 (NIV):** "For this reason a man will leave his father and mother and be united to his wife, and the two will become one flesh. This is a profound mystery, but I am talking about Christ and the church."
2.

3. **Hebrews 13:4 (NIV):** "Marriage should be honoured by all, and the marriage bed kept pure, for God will judge the adulterer and all the sexually immoral."
4. **1 Corinthians 13:4-7 (NIV):** "Love is patient, love is kind. It does not envy, it does not boast, it is not proud... It always protects, always trusts, always hopes, always perseveres."

Themes for Preparing for Marriage

- "Build your union on faith; let love guide your path."
- "A God-centred marriage is a strong foundation."
- "Commitment in Christ leads to lasting love."
- "Honour each other as you honour God."

Quotes for Reflection

1. "The best thing a couple can do for their children is to love each other." – John Wooden
2. "Marriage is not just about finding someone you can live with; it's about finding someone you can't live without." – Unknown
3. "A successful marriage requires falling in love many times, always with the same person." – Mignon McLaughlin

In contrast, non-godly marriages may lack these spiritual dimensions:

1. **Secular Focus:** These marriages may prioritise personal happiness or societal norms over spiritual commitments.
2. **Transactional Nature:** Relationships may be based on convenience or mutual benefit rather than deep emotional or spiritual connection.
3. **Lack of Accountability:** Without a shared belief system or commitment to divine principles, couples may not feel accountable for their actions towards each other.
4. **Potential for Instability:** Non-godly marriages might be more susceptible to challenges such as infidelity or divorce due to lack of strong foundational values.

1b: The Covenant of Marriage

The covenant of marriage is a sacred and binding agreement between a man and a woman, established by God, that signifies their commitment to each other for life. This covenant encompasses several key elements that define its nature, purpose, and responsibilities.

Definition of Covenant

A covenant is fundamentally different from a contract. While contracts can be broken or renegotiated, covenants are intended to be lifelong commitments that reflect an unbreakable bond. In the context of marriage, this means that both partners pledge themselves to one another in a manner that is solemn and enduring1.

Biblical Foundation

The concept of marriage as a covenant is deeply rooted in Scripture. Genesis 2:24 states, "For this reason a man will leave his father and mother and be united to his wife, and they will become one flesh." This verse illustrates the profound unity that marriage creates between two individuals2. Furthermore, throughout the Bible, God uses the imagery of covenant to describe His relationship with humanity, emphasising fidelity and commitment.

Characteristics of the Marriage Covenant

- **Lifelong Commitment**

Marriage as a covenant signifies a lifelong commitment where both partners agree to remain together until death separates them. This commitment is not contingent upon circumstances or feelings but is based on mutual promises made before God3.

- **Solemn Vows**

When entering into marriage, couples typically exchange vows that outline their intentions and promises to one another. These vows serve as verbal affirmations of their commitment and are often witnessed by family and friends4. The seriousness of these vows reflects the gravity of the marital covenant.

- **Spiritual Dimension**

The marriage covenant involves not only the couple but also God as an integral participant in the union. This divine aspect underscores the belief that God ordains marriage and should reflect His love and faithfulness5. As stated in Ephesians 5:32, "This mystery is profound; I am saying that it refers to Christ and the church," indicating that Christian marriages should mirror the relationship between Christ and His followers.

Responsibilities Within the Covenant

- **Mutual Love and Respect**

Both partners are called to love each other selflessly, prioritising each other's needs above their own (Ephesians 5:25-28). This mutual love creates an environment where both individuals feel valued and supported6.

- **Faithfulness**

Faithfulness is a cornerstone of the marriage covenant. Adultery or infidelity breaks this sacred bond and violates the promises made during the wedding ceremony7. The Bible emphasises fidelity in passages such as Proverbs 2:17 which warns against abandoning one's spouse.

CHAPTER 1: The Meaning of Marriage

- **Support Through Challenges**

Marriage can face various challenges over time; however, couples are encouraged to support each other through difficulties rather than seeking separation or divorce8. The commitment inherent in a covenant encourages spouses to work through conflicts together.

Legal Aspects of Covenant Marriage

In some jurisdictions in the United States, such as Arizona, Arkansas, and Louisiana, there exists a legal framework for what is known as "covenant marriage." This type of marriage requires couples to undergo premarital counselling and limits grounds for divorce compared to traditional marriages9. Couples must demonstrate specific reasons for divorce (e.g., adultery or abuse) rather than simply citing irreconcilable differences.

Conclusion

The covenant of marriage represents a profound commitment between two individuals before God, characterised by lifelong dedication, mutual respect, faithfulness, and support through life's challenges. Understanding this covenantal nature can help couples navigate their relationships with greater intention and purpose.

Interpretation of Covenant Marriage

Different cultures interpret the covenant of marriage in various ways, often influenced by their historical, religious, and social contexts. Below is a detailed exploration of how different cultures view marriage as a covenant, supported by biblical verses.

- **Understanding the Concept of Covenant in Marriage**

A covenant in the context of marriage is a solemn agreement that binds two individuals together for life. It is not merely a contract based on mutual benefits but a sacred commitment before God and witnesses. The biblical foundation for this understanding can be found in Genesis 2:24, which states:

"Therefore a man shall leave his father and mother and hold fast to his wife, and they shall become one flesh."

This verse emphasises the unity and permanence intended in the marriage relationship.

- **Western Cultural Interpretations**

In many Western cultures, particularly those influenced by Christianity, marriage is viewed as a sacred covenant established before God. This perspective emphasises fidelity, love, and mutual support as essential components of the marital relationship.

Example: Christian Weddings

Christian weddings often include vows that reflect this covenantal understanding. For instance, couples may say:

"I take you to be my lawfully wedded wife/husband, to have and to hold from this day forward, for better or for worse, for richer or poorer, in sickness and in health..."

These vows echo the commitment described in Malachi 2:14:

"But you say, 'Why does he not?' Because the LORD was witness between you and the wife of your youth, to whom you have been faithless..."

This highlights that God witnesses the covenant made between spouses.

- **African Cultural Interpretations**

In many African cultures, marriage is also seen as a covenant but often includes communal aspects where families play significant roles in the union.

Example: Bride Price

In several African traditions, the practice of paying a bride price (or dowry) symbolises respect for the bride's family and acknowledges her value within her community. This act can be seen as an extension of the covenant relationship where both families are involved.

Biblical support for this can be found in Exodus 22:16-17:

"If a man seduces a virgin who is not betrothed and lies with her, he shall give the bride-price for her and make his wife."

This reflects how marriage involves not just two individuals but also their families.

4. Asian Cultural Interpretations

Asian cultures often emphasise arranged marriages where families select partners based on compatibility rather than romantic love alone.

Example: Arranged Marriages

In countries like India or Japan, marriages are frequently arranged by parents who consider factors such as caste, social status, and family background. The emphasis here is on familial duty rather than individual choice.

The biblical concept of family involvement can be seen in Genesis 24 when Abraham sends his servant to find a wife for Isaac:

"And I will ask my lord's servant... If she says to me... 'Drink,' then I will know that she is the one whom you have appointed..." (Genesis 24:14).

This illustrates how family decisions play an integral role in establishing marital covenants.

- **Indigenous Cultural Interpretations**

Indigenous cultures often view marriage as part of broader spiritual beliefs connected to land and community.

CHAPTER 1: The Meaning of Marriage

Example: Spiritual Connections

For many Native American tribes, marriage ceremonies may involve rituals that honour nature spirits or ancestors. The union is seen as not only binding two individuals but also connecting them spiritually to their heritage.

The Bible reflects similar sentiments about honouring one's heritage through marriage in Deuteronomy 7:3-4:

"You shall not intermarry with them... For they would turn away your sons from following me..."

This verse underscores how marriages were meant to preserve cultural identity within God's chosen people.

Conclusion

Across different cultures, whether Western Christian traditions emphasising personal vows, African customs involving bride prices, Asian practices centred around arranged marriages, or Indigenous beliefs connecting unions with spirituality, the interpretation of marriage as a covenant remains profound. Each culture brings its unique elements while still aligning with biblical principles that highlight commitment before God and community involvement.

By understanding these diverse interpretations of marriage covenants across cultures, we gain insight into how deeply rooted values shape relationships worldwide while recognising common threads that unite us all under God's design for marital bonds.

CHAPTER 2: DIFFERENCE BETWEEN A PARTNER AND A SPOUSE

Theme Scripture:

"Can two walk together, except they are agreed?," asks Third chapter Amos: 3:3

Many have paid the price in postponement of destiny, sorrow, and suffering after mistaking a companion for a husband. Making sensible decisions in relationships starts with knowing the difference between someone who is attached to you (spouse) and someone who walks with you (partner). A spouse supports you eternally; a partner helps you briefly.

1. Definitions and variations

A. Who is a partner

- Partner: Usually referring to someone one has an intimate connection with, this phrase may not always reflect formal marriage. Though romantic or otherwise, partners can be in many other kinds of partnerships and do not necessarily have the same legal privileges or social acceptance connected with marriage. In business, friendship, or even a sexual relationship, a partner is someone you are emotionally or physically connected to for a specific purpose. It could or might not call for a covenant or pledge.
- They could back your objectives.
- They could have shared passions or interests.
- Though they might not be divinely allocated.

Illustrations include:

Delilah travelled with Samson (Judges 16:4–21). She shared enthusiasm but not direction.

B. Who qualifies as a spouse?

- A spouse is especially someone who is lawfully wedded to another individual. This word has legal ramifications on property, inheritance, healthcare choices, etc., which are not usually granted to partners unless stated by law. In covenant marriage, a spouse is someone you are divinely linked to – blessed, approved, and destined to fulfil destiny with you by God.
- A spouse eternally, emotionally, and spiritually supports you.
- A spouse is intentional and lasting, not only here-present.
- Among other things:

- Chosen by prayer and divine direction, Rebekah was Isaac's wife (Genesis 24).
- Ruth was Boaz's wife, placed by God and validated by covenant (Ruth 4:13).

2. WHY A PARTNER NOT ALWAYS A SPOUSE
- Marriage is a covenant; partnership can be seasonal.
- A spouse is sent by God; a partner is sent by feelings.
- A spouse will cover and guard you; a partner will test you.
- A partner goes into destiny with you; they may divert your attention from destiny.

3. BIBLICAL Comparisons
- Character, Partner or Spouse? Goal
- Samson and Delilah Partner Death, blindness, and treachery—Judges 16
- Comfort, covenant, and continuation of promise for Isaac and Rebekah from Genesis 24:67
- David and Michal Partner (first wife but not in line spiritually) Conflict, misinterpretation, no fruit (2 Samuel 6:20–23).
- Joseph and Mary Spouse Divine Partnership for a Specific Goal (Matthew 1:18–25)

4. Sayings TO NEVER forget
- "A companion will die with you; a partner will dance with you."
- "Don't marry Delilah simply because she seems to be destined."
- Feelings pass, but covenant endures.

5. WISDOM QUOTES
- "A partner may fit your present; only a spouse fits your future."
- "Before you say 'I do', ask God, 'Is this You?'"
- "A spouse is found in the cloud of divine instruction, not in the crowd." Chika Ugo, Pastor

6. HOW TO LEARN THE DIFFERENCE
- Before committing, pray intensely. Proverbs 3:5–6
- Check spiritual alignment with 2 Corinthians 6:14.
- See Godly Advice; Proverbs 11:14
- See fruit above emotions in Matthew 7:16.

- Wait on confirmation, not on chemistry. Psalm 27:14

7. Results of Mistaking a Partner for a Spouse
- Loss
- Delay in destiny
- Conflicts in marriage
- spiritual warfare
- regret that one could have averted

Questions for Discussions
1. Have you ever mistaken a mate for a spouse from the past?

2. Which main traits, in your opinion, are absolutely necessary for a godly partner?

3. How can one use prayer and discernment to prevent errors in future decisions?

Declared announcements
I won't confuse covenant for friendship.

God will show me my real partner at His ideal moment.

Emotional blindness cannot slow down my destiny.

I release every terrible alliance under Jesus's name.

Pray points
- Open my eyes, Lord, to see who is my husband and a partner.
- Every Delilah or Lot I travel with, Lord, disconnect me right now.
- Father, let my heart line up with Your will on a mate.
- I get grace to wait, knowledge to choose, and power to turn away dishonesty.

In summary, while all spouses can be considered partners in life, not all are spouses due to the absence of legal marital status

CHAPTER 3. CAUSES OF DIVORCE AND SINGLE MOTHERHOOD

Definitions of Divorce

Divorce is the legal dissolution of a marriage by a court or other competent body. It involves the termination of the marital union, cancelling the legal duties and responsibilities of marriage between the parties involved. The reasons for divorce can vary widely, including but not limited to irreconcilable differences, infidelity, abuse, or financial issues.

Examples of Divorce

1. **No-Fault Divorce:** This type allows either spouse to file for divorce without having to prove wrongdoing by the other party. For example, in many states in the United States of America, one spouse may simply state that the marriage has irretrievably broken down.

2. **Fault-based divorce:** In this scenario, one spouse blames the other for the breakdown of the marriage. For instance, if one partner commits adultery or engages in abusive behaviour, the other may file for divorce on those grounds.

3. **Contested vs. Uncontested Divorce:** A contested divorce occurs when spouses cannot agree on terms such as asset division or child custody, while an uncontested divorce happens when both parties reach an agreement without court intervention.

Biblical Verses on Marriage and Divorce: The Bible addresses marriage and divorce in several passages -

- Matthew 19:6 (NIV): "So they are no longer two, but one flesh. Therefore what God has joined together, let no one separate."

- Malachi 2:16 (NIV): "The man who hates and divorces his wife", says the Lord, "the God of Israel, does violence to the one he should protect."

- 1 Corinthians 7:10-11 (NIV): "To the married I give this command (not I but the Lord): A wife must not separate from her husband. But if she does, she must remain unmarried or else be reconciled to her husband."

These verses emphasise the sanctity of marriage and caution against divorce.

Quotes for Those Entering Marriage

Here are some inspirational quotes that can serve as guidance for couples preparing for marriage:

- *"Marriage is not just about finding a partner; it's about being a partner."*

- *"A successful marriage requires falling in love many times, always with the same person." — Mignon McLaughlin*
- *"Love is not about how many days, months, or years you have been together. Love is about how much you love each other every single day."*
- *"In every relationship, there will be challenges; it's how you face them together that counts."*

Divorce can occur for numerous reasons; some common causes include:

- **Communication Breakdown:** Poor communication often leads to misunderstandings that can escalate into larger conflicts (Proverbs 18:13).
- **Infidelity:** Betrayal through infidelity can severely damage trust within a marriage (Matthew 19:9).
- **Financial Issues:** Disagreements about finances are frequently cited as a significant stressor leading to divorce (1 Timothy 6:10).
- **Lack of Commitment:** When one or both partners do not fully commit to maintaining the relationship through challenges (Malachi 2:16), it increases vulnerability to separation.
- **Unresolved Conflict:** Persistent unresolved issues can lead couples toward divorce instead of reconciliation (James 1:19-20).

Causes of Single Parenthood

Single parenthood can arise from various circumstances:

1. **Divorce or Separation:** Many single parents find themselves raising children alone after a divorce or separation from their partners.
2. **Unplanned Pregnancy:** Some women become single mothers due to unexpected pregnancies without stable partnerships (Psalm 127:3).
3. **Death of a Partner:** The death of a spouse can leave a partner with children who must navigate parenting alone (1 Timothy 5:8).
4. **Choice:** Some women choose single motherhood intentionally for personal reasons or due to dissatisfaction with potential partners' qualities or behaviours.

In conclusion, understanding marriage's meaning involves recognising its multifaceted nature; spiritually significant yet also socially constructed, and acknowledging how differing values influence marital dynamics while considering contemporary issues like divorce and single parenthood.

Understanding Divorce in the Bible

Divorce is a complex and sensitive topic addressed in various parts of the Bible. The teachings emphasise the sanctity of marriage and provide guidance on divorce, reflecting God's intentions for marital relationships.

Biblical Teachings on Divorce

The Old Testament Perspectives

In the Old Testament, divorce was permitted under certain circumstances. Deuteronomy 24:1-4 states:

"If a man marries a woman who becomes displeased with him because he finds something indecent about her, and he writes her a certificate of divorce, gives it to her and sends her from his house..."

This passage indicates that while divorce was allowed, it was regulated to prevent abuse and ensure some level of protection for the divorced woman.

The New Testament Insights

In the New Testament, Jesus addresses divorce more directly. In Matthew 19:3-9, He responds to questions about divorce by emphasising God's original design for marriage:

"Haven't you read", he replied, "that at the beginning the Creator 'made them male and female' and said, 'For this reason a man will leave his father and mother and be united to his wife, and the two will become one flesh'? So they are no longer two but one flesh. Therefore what God has joined together, let no one separate."

Here, Jesus highlights that marriage is intended to be a lifelong commitment. He acknowledges that Moses allowed divorce due to people's hard hearts but reiterates that it was not part of God's original plan.

Paul's Teachings

The Apostle Paul also discusses marriage and divorce in 1 Corinthians 7:10-11:

"To the married I give this command (not I but the Lord): A wife must not separate from her husband. But if she does, she must remain unmarried or else be reconciled to her husband. And a husband must not divorce his wife."

Paul reinforces the idea that separation should be avoided whenever possible and emphasises reconciliation as an ideal outcome.

Advice for Those Entering Marriage

Key Principles

1. **Commitment**: Understand that marriage is a covenant relationship meant to last a lifetime.
2. **Communication:** open communication is vital for resolving conflicts before they escalate.

3. **Forgiveness**: Be prepared to forgive each other's shortcomings; no one is perfect.
4. **Shared Values:** Ensure alignment on core values and beliefs, as they form the foundation of your relationship.

Quotes

"Marriage is not just about finding someone you can live with; it's about finding someone you can't imagine living without."

"A successful marriage requires falling in love many times, always with the same person."

"Love is patient; love is kind." (1 Corinthians 13:4) - A reminder of how love should manifest in daily interactions.

Conclusion

Divorce is addressed in Scripture with an emphasis on its seriousness and God's desire for marriages to endure. While there are allowances made for divorce due to human imperfection, the overarching message encourages couples to strive for unity and reconciliation.

In summary, God views marriage as a sacred bond meant to last a lifetime, advising couples to approach their union with commitment, communication, forgiveness, and shared values.

Can Christians Divorce?

Yes, Christians can divorce under certain circumstances. The Bible provides specific instances where divorce is permissible, primarily focusing on issues such as infidelity and abandonment.

Biblical Grounds for Divorce

1. **Adultery**: One of the most cited reasons for divorce in Christian doctrine is adultery. In Matthew 19:9 (NIV), Jesus states, *"I tell you that anyone who divorces his wife, except for sexual immorality, and marries another woman commits adultery."* **This verse indicates that infidelity breaks the marital covenant and provides grounds for divorce.**

2. **Abandonment**: In 1 Corinthians 7:15 (NIV), Paul writes: *"But if the unbeliever leaves, let it be so. The brother or sister is not bound in such circumstances; God has called us to live in peace."* **This suggests that if an unbelieving spouse chooses to leave the marriage, the believing spouse is not obligated to remain bound to that relationship.**

3. **Emotional or Physical Abuse:** While not explicitly mentioned in scripture, many modern Christian leaders interpret biblical principles about love and respect to mean that abusive situations are grounds for separation

or divorce. Ephesians 5:25-28 emphasises mutual love and care between spouses.

Reasons Against Divorce

While there are valid reasons for divorce according to the scripture, many Christians believe that marriage should be a lifelong commitment. Here are some reasons against divorce:

1. **Covenant Commitment:** Marriage is often viewed as a sacred covenant before God. Malachi 2:16 (NIV) states, "The man who hates and divorces his wife... does violence to the one he should protect." **This verse highlights the seriousness of breaking this covenant.**

2. **Forgiveness and Reconciliation:** Many Christians emphasise forgiveness as a core principle of their faith. Matthew 6:14-15 (NIV) teaches: *"For if you forgive other people when they sin against you, your heavenly Father will also forgive you."* **This encourages couples to work through their issues rather than resort to divorce.**

3. **Witnessing Faith:** Staying together through difficulties can serve as a testimony of faith to others. Couples who endure challenges together may demonstrate God's love and grace more powerfully than those who separate.

Advice for Those Entering Marriage – Here are some guiding biblical principles and quotes for those preparing for marriage:

- **Communication:** open communication is vital in any relationship. Proverbs 18:13 (NIV) says, "To answer before listening—that is folly and shame."
- **Mutual Respect:** Ephesians 5:33 advises, "Each one of you also must love your wife as you love yourself, and the wife must respect her husband."
- **Seek Guidance:** Proverbs 15:22 (NIV) states, "Plans fail for lack of counsel, but with many advisers they succeed."

These encourage couples to seek premarital counselling or guidance from trusted mentors.

Quotes

- "Marriage is not just about finding someone you can live with; it's about finding someone you can't live without."
- "A successful marriage requires falling in love many times, always with the same person."

Conclusion

In summary, strong biblical teachings advocate for the sanctity of marriage and encourage reconciliation whenever possible, even though Christians can divorce under specific circumstances, such as adultery or abandonment. Couples entering into marriage should prepare by understanding these principles deeply.

CHAPTER 4: BIBLICAL PRINCIPLES DEFINING A SUCCESSFUL MARRIAGE

Yes, there are successful marriages. A successful marriage is characterised by mutual respect, love, effective communication, and shared goals. While every marriage is unique and faces its own challenges, many couples thrive through commitment and understanding.

Key Elements of a Successful Marriage

1. Communication: Effective communication is fundamental in any relationship. Couples who can openly discuss their feelings, concerns, and aspirations tend to have stronger bonds. This includes both verbal communication and active listening.

2. Trust: Trust forms the foundation of a healthy marriage. It involves being honest with each other and maintaining fidelity. When partners trust one another, they feel secure in their relationship.

3. Respect: Mutual respect means valuing each other's opinions, feelings, and boundaries. Couples who respect one another are more likely to support each other's personal growth.

4. Shared Goals and Values: Successful marriages often involve partners who share similar values and life goals. This alignment helps couples navigate decisions about finances, family planning, and lifestyle choices together.

5. Conflict Resolution: Disagreements are natural in any relationship; however, how couples handle conflict can determine the success of their marriage. Effective conflict resolution strategies include compromise, empathy, and finding common ground.

Examples of Successful Marriages

Good Biblical Marriages for Christians

Many times, the Bible provides models of good relationships that stress faith, commitment, and mutual respect. These are some amazing couples below, together with relevant biblical lines underlining their marriages and the principles they displayed.

1. Sarah and Abraham

Abraham's and Sarah's marriage exemplifies tenacity and faithfulness. Despite challenges including infertility and uncertain times, they remained committed to God's promises. Their story emphasises the necessity of depending on God amid difficulties.

key verse: Genesis 21:1–2 "The Lord visited Sarah as he had said, and he did to her as he had promised. And at the age God had foretold to Abraham, Sarah conceived and bore his son into old age."

2. Isaac and Rebekah

Beginning under divine guidance, Isaac and Rebekah's marriage showed trust in God's will. Particularly in tough conditions, their marriage exhibits love, respect, and encouragement of one another.

The pivotal line in Genesis 24:67 is "And Isaac brought her into the tent of Sarah his mother and took Rebekah, and she became his wife, and he loved her."

3. Ruth and Boaz

Ruth's loyalty to Naomi and Boaz's integrity produced a happy marriage, therefore securing the future of her family. Their friendship reveals compassion, respect, and God's providence in setting their meeting.

Ruth 4:13—"So Boaz took Ruth, and she became his wife." Key Verse He then entered her and the Lord confirmed her pregnancy; she carried a son.

4. Joseph and Mary

Among challenging circumstances, Mary and Joseph paid God great reverence. Their openness to embrace God's will for their existence exposes the real character of marriage.

"When Joseph woke from sleep, he did as the angel of the Lord commanded him: he took his wife but knew her not until she had given birth to a son." Key Verse

5. Priscilla and Aquila.

Priscilla and Aquila were partners in ministry, therefore demonstrating a religious journey together in addition to their marriage. Like they motivated each other spiritually, they served the early church.

Act 18:26, *"He began to speak boldly in the synagogue, but when Priscilla and Aquila heard him, they took him aside and explained to him the way of God more precisely."*

finally

These biblical pictures highlight how strong relationships are defined by loyalty, mutual respect, love, patience, and a devotion to God's plan. Though each couple faced unique challenges, they discovered guidance from their faith in God.

Christian marriages can provide strong images of commitment, love, and dedication. The above are several Biblical couples whose relationships reflect successful marriages, in addition to relevant scripture lines stressing their qualities and the principles they stood for.

Biblical Perspectives on Marriage

The Bible offers numerous verses that emphasise the importance of love, respect, and unity in marriage:

- **Ephesians 5:25:** "Husbands, love your wives, just as Christ loved the church."
- **1 Corinthians 13:4-7:** "Love is patient; love is kind... It always protects, always trusts, always hopes, always perseveres."

These verses highlight the virtues that contribute to a lasting marital relationship.

Quotes for Marriage: These inspirational quotes can guide those entering into marriage:

"A successful marriage requires falling in love many times, always with the same person." — Mignon McLaughlin

"Marriage is not about finding someone you can live with; it's about finding someone you can't live without." — Rafael Ortiz

These quotes remind couples of the ongoing effort required to maintain a loving relationship.

Conclusion

In summary, successful marriages do exist when built on communication, trust, respect, shared goals, and effective conflict resolution. By adhering to these principles and drawing inspiration from biblical teachings and wise sayings, couples can foster enduring relationships.

Biblical principles that define a successful marriage include:

Covenant Commitment: Marriage is viewed as a sacred covenant established by God between one man and one woman. This commitment is lifelong and reflects God's faithfulness to His people. The Bible emphasises that no one should separate what God has joined together (Mark 10:9) and highlights the importance of faithfulness in this covenant (Malachi 2:14).

Unity and Oneness: Genesis 2:24 states, "Therefore a man shall leave his father and mother and hold fast to his wife, and they shall become one flesh." This principle underscores the idea of unity, where both partners are to work towards becoming one in purpose, spirit, and intimacy.

Mutual Love and Sacrifice: Ephesians 5:25 instructs husbands to love their wives as Christ loved the church, which involves self-sacrificial love. Wives are also called to respect their husbands (Ephesians 5:33). This mutual love creates an environment where both partners prioritise each other's needs above their own.

Communication and Support: Effective communication is vital for a successful marriage. Ephesians 4:29 encourages spouses to speak words that build each other up. Additionally, Ecclesiastes 4:9-12 highlights the importance of companionship and support, stating that two are better than one because they can help each other.

Purpose of Procreation: The Bible teaches that part of God's design for marriage includes procreation (Genesis 1:28). Couples are encouraged to raise children in a godly manner, nurturing them in the faith.

Spiritual Growth Together: A successful marriage involves both partners growing spiritually together through prayer, studying Scripture, and serving others (Matthew 18:20). This shared spiritual journey strengthens their bond.

Conflict Resolution with Grace: The Bible provides guidance on resolving conflicts with grace and humility (Philippians 4:2-3). Couples are encouraged to forgive each other as Christ forgave them (Colossians 3:13).

CHAPTER 5: DIFFERENCES FROM SECULAR VIEWS ON MARRIAGE

Contrary to biblical principles, secular views on marriage often emphasise the following aspects:

1. **Contractual Agreement:** Secular perspectives typically view marriage as a legal contract between two individuals rather than a sacred covenant ordained by God. This view may prioritise personal happiness or fulfilment over spiritual commitments.

2. **Individualism Over Unity:** Secular views may focus more on individual desires and personal growth rather than the concept of becoming one flesh or working towards common goals as a couple.

3. **Emphasis on Personal Happiness:** Many secular approaches suggest that if individuals are not happy in their marriage, they have the right to leave or seek alternative arrangements, such as open marriages or cohabitation without commitment.

4. **Lack of Spiritual Foundation:** Secular views often do not incorporate spiritual growth or religious practices into the marital relationship, which can lead to couples lacking shared values or purpose beyond personal satisfaction.

5. **Flexible Definitions of Marriage:** The secular worldview allows for various forms of relationships beyond traditional heterosexual marriages, including same-sex unions or non-monogamous arrangements without adhering to biblical definitions.

6. **Focus on Emotional Fulfilment:** While emotional connection is important in both views, secular perspectives may prioritise feelings over commitments made during marriage vows, leading to higher divorce rates when emotions change.

7. **Conflict Resolution Based on Personal Values:** In secular counselling approaches, conflict resolution might rely more on psychological theories than on biblical teachings about forgiveness and grace.

Understanding these biblical principles alongside secular views on marriage enables couples to navigate their relationships with clarity regarding their values and expectations while creating a deeper connection rooted in faith.

CHAPTER 6: CHRISTIAN TEACHINGS ON LOVE AND COMMITMENT

Understanding Love and Commitment in Marriage

Love and commitment are foundational elements of a successful marriage. Love is often described as a deep affection, care, and connection between partners, while commitment refers to the dedication and promise to maintain that relationship through all circumstances. Together, they create a strong bond that can withstand challenges and foster growth.

Examples of Love in Marriage

1. **Acts of Kindness:** Regularly expressing appreciation for your partner through small gestures, such as leaving notes or preparing their favourite meal.

2. **Emotional Support:** Being there for each other during tough times, listening actively, and providing comfort.

3. **Quality Time:** Prioritising time together without distractions to strengthen your emotional connection.

Examples of Commitment in Marriage

1. **Faithfulness:** Staying loyal to one another emotionally and physically throughout the marriage.

2. **Shared Goals:** Working together towards common objectives, such as financial stability or family planning.

3. **Conflict Resolution:** Committing to resolve disagreements respectfully and constructively rather than allowing them to fester.

Bible Verses About Love and Commitment

- **1 Corinthians 13:4-7:** "Love is patient, love is kind. It does not envy, it does not boast, it is not proud. It does not dishonour others, it is not self-seeking, it is not easily angered, it keeps no record of wrongs."

- **Ephesians 5:25:** "Husbands, love your wives, just as Christ loved the church and gave himself up for her."

- **Genesis 2:24:** "Therefore a man shall leave his father and mother and hold fast to his wife, and they shall become one flesh."

- **Colossians 3:14:** "And over all these virtues put on love, which binds them all together in perfect unity."

- **Romans 13:8:** "Owe no one anything except to love each other, for the one who loves another has fulfilled the law."

Sayings About Love and Commitment
1. "Together Forever: In Love and Commitment."
2. "Love Deeply; Commit Fully."
3. "Two Hearts, One Promise".
4. "Building a Life Together with Love."
5. "Commitment is the Heartbeat of Marriage."

Quotes on Love and Commitment
"The best thing to hold onto in life is each other." — Audrey Hepburn

"A successful marriage requires falling in love many times, always with the same person." — Mignon McLaughlin

"Love doesn't make the world go round; love is what makes the ride worthwhile." — Franklin P. Jones

"Commitment unlocks the doors of imagination, allowing vision to take flight." — James Womack

"True love stands by each other's side on good days and stands even closer on bad days." — Unknown

Understanding these principles of love and commitment along with relevant scriptures, sayings, and quotes will help couples to prepare themselves for a fulfilling marriage groan.

Christian Teachings on love and commitment
Christian teachings on love and commitment shape marital relationships by emphasising the sacred, covenantal nature of marriage, which is rooted in mutual sacrifice, faithfulness, and a divine purpose. In contrast, modern secular beliefs often view marriage as a social contract focused on personal happiness and individual fulfilment.

Step 1: Understanding Christian Teachings on Love and Commitment

Christian teachings emphasise that marriage is a sacred covenant established by God between one man and one woman. This perspective is grounded in biblical principles that highlight several key aspects:

1. **Covenantal Nature:** Christian marriage is seen as a lifelong commitment that reflects the relationship between Christ and the Church (Ephesians 5:31-32). This covenantal view promotes the idea that spouses are bound not just by legal agreements but by spiritual promises to each other and to God.

2. **Mutual Sacrifice:** The concept of love in Christian teachings involves selflessness and sacrificial giving. Ephesians 5:25 instructs husbands to

love their wives as Christ loved the Church, which includes putting their spouse's needs above their own.

3. **Faithfulness**: Faithfulness is a core tenet of Christian marriage, where both partners are expected to remain loyal to each other emotionally, physically, and spiritually (Proverbs 3:3). This commitment fosters trust and security within the relationship.

4. **Divine Purpose**: Marriage is viewed as part of God's plan for human flourishing, with an emphasis on companionship, support, procreation, and reflecting God's love to others (Genesis 1:28; Ecclesiastes 4:9-12).

Step 2: Exploring Modern Secular Beliefs about Marriage

In contrast to Christian teachings, modern secular beliefs about marriage often focus on individualism and personal satisfaction:

1. **Social Contract:** Many people view marriage primarily as a legal agreement, or social contract, that formalises a partnership between two consenting individuals. This perspective may favour legal rights over spiritual commitments.

2. **Personal Happiness:** Secular views often emphasise that personal happiness is the primary goal of marriage. Couples may enter into relationships seeking emotional fulfilment or companionship without necessarily considering long-term commitments or sacrifices.

3. **Flexibility in Commitment:** Modern secular beliefs may allow for more flexible definitions of commitment, including open marriages or cohabitation without formalising the relationship through marriage. This can lead to an emphasis on convenience rather than enduring loyalty.

4. **Evolving Norms:** Secular perspectives tend to adapt more readily to changing social norms regarding relationships, including acceptance of divorce as a common solution when couples face difficulties or feel unfulfilled.

Step 3: Comparing Outcomes

The differences in these foundational beliefs can lead to varied outcomes in marital relationships:

1. **Stability vs. Instability:** Christian marriages grounded in covenantal commitments often report higher levels of stability due to shared values around faithfulness and mutual sacrifice. In contrast, secular marriages may experience higher rates of divorce due to shifting priorities toward personal happiness.

2. **Emotional Depth vs. Superficiality:** The depth of emotional connection fostered by mutual sacrifice in Christian marriages can lead to stronger bonds over time, compared to some secular relationships that might prioritise immediate gratification over long-term growth.

3. **Shared Purpose vs. Individual Goals:** Couples who embrace Christian teachings often work together toward shared spiritual goals and values, enhancing their partnership's sense of purpose beyond mere coexistence or personal satisfaction.

Conclusion

In summary, Christian teachings on love and commitment shape marital relationships by emphasising the sacredness of the union through mutual sacrifice, faithfulness, and divine purpose, while modern secular beliefs tend to focus more on individual happiness and flexibility within partnerships. These differing foundations significantly influence how couples navigate challenges within their marriages and define success in their relationships.

CHAPTER 7: BEST WAYS TO FOSTER UNITY IN MARRIAGES SUPPORTED BY BIBLE VERSES

Promoting unity in marriage is essential for a healthy and lasting relationship. The Bible provides numerous teachings that can guide couples in building a strong, unified partnership. Below are some effective ways to strengthen unity in marriages, along with corresponding biblical verses that support these principles.

Open Communication: Importance of Dialogue

Open communication refers to the practice of sharing thoughts, feelings, and concerns in a transparent and honest manner. It involves active listening, empathy, and a willingness to engage in dialogue without fear of judgement or retaliation. In the context of marriage, open communication is essential for building trust, resolving conflicts, and fostering intimacy between partners.

Importance of Dialogue in Marriage

1. **Building Trust:** Open communication helps establish trust between partners. When both individuals feel safe expressing their thoughts and emotions, it strengthens their bond and creates a secure environment for the relationship to flourish.

2. **Conflict Resolution:** Every relationship encounters disagreements. Open dialogue allows couples to address issues constructively rather than allowing resentment to build up. By discussing problems openly, partners can work together to find solutions that satisfy both parties.

3. **Emotional Intimacy:** Sharing feelings and experiences builds emotional closeness. Couples who communicate openly are more likely to understand each other's needs and desires, leading to a deeper connection and bonding.

4. **Preventing Misunderstandings:** Clear communication reduces the likelihood of misunderstandings that can lead to conflict. By articulating thoughts clearly and checking for understanding, couples can avoid unnecessary disputes.

5. **Encouraging Growth:** Open dialogue encourages personal growth within the relationship. Partners can share their aspirations and support each other's goals, which contributes to individual fulfilment as well as collective happiness.

Bible Verses on Communication

The following Bible verses emphasise the importance of communication in relationships:

- **Ephesians 4:29 (NIV):** "Do not let any unwholesome talk come out of your mouths, but only what is helpful for building others up according to their needs, that it may benefit those who listen."
- **James 1:19 (NIV):** "My dear brothers and sisters, take note of this: Everyone should be quick to listen, slow to speak and slow to become angry."
- **Proverbs 15:1 (NIV):** "A gentle answer turns away wrath, but a harsh word stirs up anger."

These verses illustrate the importance of thoughtful communication that promotes understanding and harmony.

Quotes on Open Communication

The following sayings and quotes encapsulate the essence of open communication in marriage:

"Communication is key; unlock your hearts."

"Talk it out before you walk it out."

"In marriage, silence is not golden; it's dangerous."

"Listen with the intent to understand, not just respond."

"Words are powerful; use them wisely."

These sayings serve as reminders for couples about the necessity of maintaining open lines of communication throughout their marriage journey.

Effective communication is the cornerstone of any successful marriage. Couples should strive to express their thoughts and feelings openly while also listening actively to each other.

Biblical Support

- **James 1:19**: "My dear brothers and sisters, take note of this: Everyone should be quick to listen, slow to speak and slow to become angry." This verse emphasises the importance of listening to and understanding each other.

Conclusion

In summary, open communication is vital for a successful marriage as it fosters trust, resolves conflicts effectively, enhances emotional intimacy, prevents misunderstandings, and encourages personal growth within the partnership. Biblical teachings further reinforce these principles by advocating for respectful dialogue that builds one another up.

2. Shared Goals and Values : Identifying Common Ground

Shared goals and values are fundamental to a successful marriage. They provide a common foundation that helps couples navigate challenges, make decisions, and grow together. Here are some Bible verses and quotes that emphasise the importance of shared goals and values for those entering into marriage:

Bible Verses

1. **Amos 3:3** – "Do two walk together unless they have agreed to meet?" This verse highlights the necessity of agreement in a relationship, emphasising that shared goals are essential for unity.

2. **Philippians 2:2** – "Complete my joy by being of the same mind, having the same love, being in full accord and of one mind." This scripture encourages couples to align their thoughts and affections, promoting harmony through shared values.

3. **Ecclesiastes 4:9-10** – "Two are better than one because they have a good reward for their toil. For if they fall, one will lift up his fellow." This passage illustrates how shared goals can enhance support and collaboration in marriage.

4. **Matthew 18:19-20** – "Again I say to you, if two of you agree on earth about anything they ask, it will be done for them by my Father in heaven." This verse emphasises the power of agreement in prayer and life decisions when partners share common goals.

5. **Colossians 3:14** - "And above all these put on love, which binds everything together in perfect harmony." Love is essential for maintaining unity around shared values and goals within marriage.

Words of affirmations

- **"Together We Thrive"** – A reminder that mutual support leads to growth as a couple.

- **"United in Purpose"** – Emphasises the strength found in having aligned objectives.

- **"Building Dreams Together"** – Highlights the collaborative aspect of achieving personal and joint aspirations.

- **"One Heart, One Vision"** suggests that true partnership involves sharing both emotional connection and future plans.

Quotes

- "A successful marriage requires falling in love many times, always with the same person." – **Mignon McLaughlin**. This quote reflects the ongoing commitment to nurturing shared feelings and goals throughout marriage.

- "Marriage is not just about finding someone you can live with; it's about finding someone you can't imagine living without." – **Unknown**. It underscores the depth of connection needed to pursue shared dreams effectively.

- "In every great marriage, there are two people who have chosen to love each other unconditionally." – **Unknown**. This quote highlights that unconditional love is rooted in shared values that guide actions and decisions.

- "The best thing to hold onto in life is each other." – **Audrey Hepburn** A reminder that mutual support is crucial when pursuing common goals together.

- "Love doesn't make the world go round; love is what makes the ride worthwhile." – **Franklin P. Jones**. This quote emphasises that while love is vital, having shared aspirations enhances the journey through life together.

Couples should work together to identify shared goals and values that strengthen their bond. This could include spiritual goals, family aspirations, or financial objectives.

Biblical Support

- **Amos 3:3:** "Do two walk together unless they have agreed to do so?" This verse highlights the importance of unity in purpose and direction within a marriage.

Through attention to these biblical principles, complemented by motivational phrases and quotations, engaged couples can establish a strong foundation rooted in shared goals and values, providing lifelong guidance for their marriage.

3. Mutual Respect: Valuing Each Other

Mutual respect in the context of marriage refers to the recognition and appreciation of each partner's worth, feelings, and opinions. It involves treating each other with dignity, valuing one another's perspectives, and creating an environment where both partners feel safe to express themselves. This foundational principle is essential for a healthy and lasting relationship, as it encourages open communication, understanding, and support.

Bible Verses on Mutual Respect

The Bible provides numerous verses that emphasise the importance of respect within relationships, particularly in marriage. Here are some key scriptures:

1. **Ephesians 5:33:** "However, let each one of you love his wife as himself, and let the wife see that she respects her husband." This verse highlights the reciprocal nature of love and respect in marriage.
2. **Philippians 2:3-4:** "Do nothing from selfish ambition or conceit, but in humility count others more significant than yourselves. Let each of you look not only to his own interests but also to the interests of others." This passage encourages couples to prioritise each other's needs and well-being.
3. **1 Peter 3:7:** "Likewise, husbands, live with your wives in an understanding way, showing honour to the woman as the weaker vessel since they are heirs with you of the grace of life." This verse underscores the importance of honouring and respecting one's spouse.
4. **Colossians 3:18-19:** "Wives, submit to your husbands, as is fitting in the Lord. Husbands, love your wives and do not be harsh with them." Here, mutual respect is framed within the context of love and care.

Sayings Emphasising Mutual Respect

Sayings can serve as powerful reminders for couples entering marriage about the significance of mutual respect:

- "Respect is the foundation; love is its expression."
- "In our union, we honour each other's voice."
- "Together we rise by lifting each other up."
- "Respect fuels our love; love nurtures our respect."

Quotes About Mutual Respect

Here are some insightful quotes that reflect on mutual respect in relationships:

- "A great marriage is not when the 'perfect couple' comes together. It is when an imperfect couple learns to enjoy their differences." – Dave Meurer
- "Mutual respect is essential for a successful partnership." – Unknown
- "Love recognises no barriers; it jumps hurdles, leaps fences, and penetrates walls to arrive at its destination full of hope." – Maya Angelou
- "True love cannot be found where it does not exist, nor can it be denied where it does." – Torquato Tasso

Respecting one another's opinions, feelings, and individuality is crucial for engendering unity. Couples should appreciate their differences as strengths rather than weaknesses.

Biblical Support

- **Ephesians 5:33:** "Each one of you also must love his wife as he loves himself, and the wife must respect her husband." This verse underscores the mutual respect that should exist between partners.

Incorporating these principles into their relationship from the outset helps couples build a strong foundation based on mutual respect that will support them throughout their marriage journey.

4. Forgiveness

Definition of Forgiveness in Marriage

Forgiveness is a fundamental principle in marriage, emphasising the act of letting go of resentment and granting pardon to one's spouse for wrongdoing. In the context of the Bible, forgiveness is not merely an emotional release but a spiritual commitment to restoring relationships. It involves recognising that both partners are imperfect and will inevitably hurt each other at some point. The essence of forgiveness is rooted in love, mercy, and grace, reflecting how God forgives humanity.

Bible Verses on Forgiveness for Marriage

1. **Colossians 3:13:** "Bear with each other and forgive one another if any of you has a grievance against someone. Forgive as the Lord forgave you." This verse highlights the importance of mutual forgiveness in marriage and encourages couples to emulate God's forgiveness towards them.

2. **Ephesians 4:31-32:** "Get rid of all bitterness, rage and anger, brawling and slander, along with every form of malice. Be kind and compassionate to one another, forgiving each other, just as in Christ God forgave you." This passage emphasises that kindness and compassion should govern marital relationships, promoting a culture of forgiveness.

3. **Matthew 6:14-15:** "For if you forgive others their trespasses, your heavenly Father will also forgive you; but if you do not forgive others their trespasses, neither will your Father forgive your trespasses." This scripture underscores the reciprocal nature of forgiveness—highlighting its necessity for spiritual health within marriage.

4. **1 Peter 4:8:** "Above all, keep loving one another earnestly, since love covers a multitude of sins." Love serves as the foundation for forgiveness; it encourages couples to overlook faults and extend grace.

5. **Mark 11:25:** "And whenever you stand praying, forgive if you have anything against anyone, so that your Father also, who is in heaven, may forgive you your trespasses." This verse connects prayer with forgiveness, suggesting that maintaining

a forgiving heart is essential for spiritual communion.

Sayings About Forgiveness in Marriage

- "Forgive Freely; Love Deeply."
- "In Every Conflict Lies an Opportunity for Forgiveness."
- "Forgiveness Is the Key to Lasting Love."
- "Choose Forgiveness Over Resentment."
- "Together We Rise by Letting Go."

Quotes on Forgiveness for Couples

1. "A happy marriage is the union of two good forgivers." — Ruth Bell Graham
   This quote encapsulates the idea that successful marriages thrive on mutual forgiveness.
2. "To err is human; to forgive divine." — Alexander Pope
   Alexander Pope serves as a reminder that everyone makes mistakes and that forgiving others is a noble act.
3. "Forgiveness does not change the past, but it does enlarge the future." — Paul Boese
   This quote emphasises how forgiveness can transform relationships in the future.
4. "Forgiveness is not an occasional act; it is a constant attitude." — Martin Luther King Jr.
   Martin Luther King Jr. highlighted that maintaining a forgiving spirit should be integral to marital life.
5. "When we give ourselves permission to be imperfect, we discover our true selves—and we can begin to forgive ourselves and others." — Brené Brown
   Brené Brown encourages couples to embrace imperfection as part of their journey together.

Letting Go of Grudges

Forgiveness is vital for maintaining harmony in a marriage. Couples must learn to forgive each other for mistakes and shortcomings.

Biblical Support

- **Colossians 3:13:** "Bear with each other and forgive one another if any of you has a grievance against someone. Forgive as the Lord forgave you." This verse encourages couples to practice forgiveness as a means to foster unity.

These biblical principles, when integrated into their daily lives before entering marriage, allow couples to cultivate an environment where love flourishes through understanding and forgiveness.

- **Prayer Together : Spiritual Connection**

Understanding the Meaning of Praying Together as a Couple

Praying together as a couple is a spiritual practice that fosters intimacy, strengthens the bond between partners, and aligns their values and goals. This act of sharing prayer can enhance communication, deepen emotional connections, and provide mutual support in navigating life's challenges.

- **Spiritual Connection**

When couples pray together, they engage in a shared spiritual experience that can lead to greater understanding and empathy for one another. This practice allows partners to express their hopes, fears, and gratitude collectively. It encourages vulnerability and openness, which are essential for a healthy relationship.

- **Strengthening the Relationship**

Couples who pray together often report feeling more connected to each other. Prayer can serve as a reminder of their commitment to one another and their shared faith. It helps couples to focus on their relationship with God while also nurturing their bond with each other.

- **Guidance and Support**

Prayer provides couples with guidance during difficult times. By seeking divine assistance together, they can find strength in their faith and reassurance that they are not alone in facing challenges. This shared reliance on faith can help couples navigate conflicts more effectively.

Bible Verses About Prayer in Marriage

Here are some relevant Bible verses that emphasise the importance of prayer in marriage.

1. Matthew 18:20 – "For where two or three gather in my name, there am I with them."
2. Philippians 4:6-7 – "Do not be anxious about anything, but in every situation, by prayer and petition, with thanksgiving, present your requests to God."
3. 1 Thessalonians 5:16-18 – "Rejoice always, pray continually, give thanks in all circumstances; for this is God's will for you in Christ Jesus."

These verses drive home the importance of coming together in prayer and maintaining an attitude of gratitude and connection with God.

Slogans and Quotes for Couples Preparing for Marriage

Here are some inspirational slogans and quotes that can encourage couples

about to enter marriage:
- "A couple that prays together stays together."
- "In unity there is strength; let prayer be your foundation."
- "Together we seek His guidance; together we grow."
- "Love is patient; love is kind; through prayer we align."

These phrases encapsulate the essence of partnership built on faith and mutual support. Praying together strengthens the spiritual bond between spouses and invites divine guidance into their relationship.

Biblical Support

Matthew 18:20: "For where two or three gather in my name, there am I with them." This verse reassures couples that God is present when they come together in prayer.

Conclusion

In summary, praying together as a couple means engaging in a shared spiritual practice that enhances emotional intimacy, strengthens relationships, provides guidance during challenges, and fosters a deeper connection with God. Couples preparing for marriage can benefit from incorporating prayer into their daily lives, as it lays a strong foundation for their future together.

6. Quality Time Together: Prioritising Relationship

Understanding Quality Time Together as a Couple

Quality time together as a couple refers to the intentional and meaningful moments spent between partners that foster connection, communication, and intimacy. This concept emphasises the importance of being fully present with one another, engaging in activities that both partners enjoy, and creating shared experiences that strengthen their bonds.

Importance of Quality Time

1. **Strengthening Relationships:** Spending quality time together allows couples to deepen their understanding of each other. It helps build trust and emotional intimacy, which are crucial for a healthy relationship.

2. **Communication:** Engaging in conversations during quality time can improve communication skills. Couples learn to express their thoughts and feelings openly, which is vital for resolving conflicts and enhancing mutual respect.

3. **Shared Experiences:** Participating in activities together, whether it's cooking, hiking, or simply watching a movie, creates memories that couples can cherish. These shared experiences contribute to a sense of

partnership and teamwork.

4. **Stress Relief:** Quality time can serve as an escape from daily stressors. It provides an opportunity for couples to relax and enjoy each other's company without distractions.

Biblical Perspectives on Quality Time

The Bible emphasises the significance of relationships and spending time together. Here are some relevant verses:

- **Ecclesiastes 4:9-12 (NIV):** "Two are better than one because they have a good return for their labour: If either of them falls down, one can help the other up."
- **1 Corinthians 13:4-7 (NIV):** "Love is patient, love is kind... It always protects, always trusts, always hopes, always perseveres." This passage highlights the qualities essential for nurturing relationships through quality time.
- **Ephesians 5:25 (NIV):** "Husbands, love your wives, just as Christ loved the church and gave himself up for her." This verse underscores the importance of selfless love and commitment in marriage.

Slogans and Quotes About Marriage

Here are some slogans and quotes that emphasise the value of quality time in marriage:

- "Together is a wonderful place to be."
- "In marriage, it's not about finding someone you can live with; it's about finding someone you can't live without."
- "The best gift you can give your partner is your time."
- "Quality over quantity—spend meaningful moments together."

Advice for Those About to Marry

- **Prioritise Each Other:** Make it a habit to set aside regular time for each other amidst busy schedules.
- **Be Present:** When spending time together, minimise distractions such as phones or television to fully engage with one another.
- **Explore New Activities:** Try new things together to keep the relationship exciting and create lasting memories.
- **Communicate Openly:** Use your quality time to discuss feelings, aspirations, and concerns openly with each other.
- **Practice Gratitude:** Regularly express appreciation for one another during your shared moments; this fosters positivity in the relationship.

By focusing on these aspects of quality time together as a couple, individuals preparing for marriage can lay a strong foundation for their future relationship.

Spending quality time together helps couples nurture their relationship amidst life's distractions. Engaging in activities they both enjoy can enhance their connection.

Biblical Support

Ecclesiastes 4:9-10: "Two are better than one because they have a good return for their labour; if either of them falls down, one can help the other up." This passage emphasises the benefits of companionship and support in marriage.

Conclusion

By implementing these strategies, such as open communication, shared goals and values, mutual respect, forgiveness, praying together, and spending quality time, couples can effectively encourage unity in their marriages based on biblical teachings. These principles not only strengthen their relationship but also align with God's design for marital harmony.

CHAPTER 8: 12 ESSENTIAL THINGS TO HELP COUPLES GROW TOGETHER IN CHRIST

Growing together in faith is vital for couples who wish to strengthen their relationship and deepen their spiritual connection. Here are twelve essential practices that can help couples grow together in Christ, along with relevant Bible verses to support each practice.

1. Praying Together

Praying together creates intimacy and invites God into the relationship. It allows couples to share their hearts, concerns, and gratitude.

Biblical Verse

"And when two or three gather in my name, there I am with them." (Matthew 18:20)

2. Studying the Bible Together

Regularly studying Scripture helps couples understand God's will and grow spiritually as a unit. It also provides guidance for navigating life's challenges.

Biblical Verse

"Your word is a lamp for my feet, a light on my path." (Psalm 119:105)

3. Attending Church Together

Participating in communal worship strengthens the couple's bond and connects them with a broader community of believers.

Biblical Verse

"Let us not give up meeting together, as some are in the habit of doing, but let us encourage one another." (Hebrews 10:25)

4. Serving Others Together

Engaging in service projects or ministry work together cultivates compassion and reinforces shared values while fulfilling Christ's command to love others.

Biblical Verse

"For even the Son of Man did not come to be served but to serve." (Mark 10:45)

5. Setting Spiritual Goals

Establishing spiritual goals encourages accountability and growth within the relationship. Couples can discuss what they hope to achieve spiritually over time.]

Biblical Verse

"Commit your work to the Lord, and your plans will be established." (Proverbs 16:3)

6. Practising Forgiveness

Forgiveness is vital to sustaining harmony in any relationship. Couples should strive to forgive each other as Christ forgives them.

Biblical Verse

"Be kind and compassionate to one another, forgiving each other, just as in Christ God forgave you" (Ephesians 4:32)

7. Cultivating Gratitude

Expressing gratitude towards one another fosters positivity and appreciation within the marriage, helping couples focus on their blessings rather than challenges.

Biblical Verse

"Give thanks in all circumstances, for this is God's will for you in Christ Jesus." (1 Thessalonians 5:18)

8. Encouraging Each Other Spiritually

Couples should uplift one another by sharing encouraging words or scriptures that inspire faith and perseverance during difficult times.

Biblical Verse

"Therefore encourage one another and build each other up." (1 Thessalonians 5:11)

9. Creating a Family Mission Statement

A family mission statement rooted in biblical principles provides direction and purpose for the couple's life together, aligning their goals with God's vision.

Biblical Verse

"But as for me and my household, we will serve the Lord." (Joshua 24:15b)

10. Celebrating Milestones Together

Recognising significant moments such as anniversaries or spiritual achievements strengthens bonds and creates lasting memories centred around faith.

Biblical Verse

"Rejoice with those who rejoice; mourn with those who mourn." (Romans 12:15)

11. Seeking Spiritual Mentorship

Finding mentors who can provide guidance based on biblical wisdom helps couples navigate challenges while growing closer to God together.

Biblical Verse

"Plans fail for lack of counsel, but with many advisers they succeed." (Proverbs 15:22)

12. Creating Open Communication About Faith

Discussing beliefs openly allows couples to understand each other's perspectives better while addressing doubts or questions that may arise along their journey.

Biblical Verse

"Let every person be quick to hear, slow to speak, slow to anger." (James 1:19)

Conclusion

By incorporating these twelve essential practices into their lives, couples can effectively grow together in Christ's support while deepening their faith individually and collectively. These actions strengthen their relationship and enhance their spiritual journeys aligned with biblical teachings.

CHAPTER 9: FACTORS CONTRIBUTING TO MARITAL FAILURE

Marriages can fail for a variety of reasons, and understanding these factors can help couples navigate their relationships more effectively. Below is a detailed list of 12 common issues that contribute to marital failure, along with advice for new couples on how to avoid these pitfalls, supported by relevant biblical verses.

1. Poor Communication

Lack of effective communication often leads to misunderstandings and resentment. Couples may struggle to express their feelings or listen actively to each other.

Advice

New couples should prioritise open and honest communication. Regularly check in with each other about feelings, expectations, and concerns.

Biblical Support

James 1:19 advises, "Everyone should be quick to listen, slow to speak and slow to become angry." This verse emphasises the importance of listening during communication.

2. Lack of Trust

What is trust? Definition of Trust

Trust is generally defined as an assured reliance on the character, ability, strength, or truth of someone or something. It encompasses a belief that another person will act consistent with expectations and is characterised by a willingness to become vulnerable to another party (the trustee) based on the presumption that they will act in ways that benefit the trustor. This relationship often involves placing resources at the disposal of another without any legal commitment from them, indicating a level of confidence and expectation for reciprocity in actions.

Components of Trust

1. **Assured Reliance:** Trust involves a strong belief in someone's reliability or integrity.

2. **Vulnerability:** The trustor willingly exposes themselves to potential risks by relying on the trustee's actions.

3. **Expectation of Benefit:** There is an inherent expectation that the trustee will act in the best interest of the trustor.

Types of Trust

Trust can also refer to a legal arrangement where one party (the trustee) holds property or assets for the benefit of another party (the beneficiary). The legal definition includes various types, such as:

- **Living Trusts:** These are established during a person's lifetime.
- **Testamentary Trusts:** Created through a will after death.
- **Revocable and Irrevocable Trusts:** Depending on whether changes can be made after establishment.

Trust issues can arise from past experiences or insecurities, leading to suspicion and conflict within the marriage.

Advice

Build trust through transparency and honesty. Be reliable and consistent in your actions and words.

Building Trust in a Relationship

Trust is a fundamental component of any healthy relationship. It builds intimacy, security, and mutual respect. Here are some detailed steps couples can take to build and maintain trust:

1. Transparency and Honesty

Transparency involves being open about your thoughts, feelings, and actions. This means sharing important information with your partner and not hiding anything that could affect the relationship.

- **Communicate openly:** regularly discuss your feelings, concerns, and experiences. This can prevent misunderstandings and build a deeper connection.
- **Be honest:** always tell the truth, even when it's difficult. Honesty lays the groundwork for trust.

Quote: "Honesty is the first chapter in the book of wisdom." – Thomas Jefferson

2. Reliability and Consistency

Being reliable means that your partner can count on you to follow through on promises and commitments.

- **Keep your promises:** if you say you will do something, make sure to follow through. This shows that you value your partner's trust.
- **Be consistent in your actions:** Your behaviour should align with your words. Inconsistencies can lead to doubt and insecurity.

Quote: "Trust is built with consistency." – Lincoln Chafee

3. Active Listening

Listening actively means fully concentrating on what your partner is saying without planning your response while they speak.

- **Show empathy:** Validate their feelings by acknowledging them, which demonstrates that you care about their perspective.
- **Ask questions:** Clarifying what they mean shows that you are engaged and interested in understanding their viewpoint.

Quote: "The most important thing in communication is hearing what isn't said." – Peter Drucker

4. Addressing Issues Promptly

When conflicts arise, addressing them quickly prevents resentment from building up.

- **Discuss problems openly:** Avoid letting issues fester; instead, talk about them as they arise.
- **Use "I" statements:** Express how you feel without blaming or criticising your partner (e.g., "I feel hurt when...").

Quote: "The greatest problem in communication is we do not listen to understand. We often listen just to reply." – Anonymous

5. Building Emotional Intimacy

Emotional intimacy strengthens trust by creating a safe space for vulnerability.

- **Share personal experiences:** Open up about past experiences that shaped who you are today.
- **Support each other's dreams:** Encourage each other's goals and aspirations, showing that you care about each other's happiness.

Quote: "Intimacy is the capacity to be rather weird with someone and find that that's okay with them." – Alain de Botton

Biblical Support

Proverbs 3:5-6 says, "Trust in the Lord with all your heart and lean not on your own understanding; in all your ways submit to him, and he will make your paths straight." Trust is foundational for any relationship.

3. Financial Disagreements

Financial disagreements in marriages refer to conflicts that arise between partners regarding money management, spending habits, savings, investments, and financial goals. These disagreements can stem from differing values, priorities, and communication styles related to finances.

Causes of Financial Disagreements

1. **Differing Spending Habits:** One partner may be a spender while the other is a saver. This fundamental difference can lead to conflicts over budgeting and expenditures.

2. **Income Disparities:** When one partner earns significantly more than the other, it can create feelings of resentment or inadequacy, leading to disputes about financial contributions and responsibilities.

3. **Financial Goals:** Partners may have different visions for their financial future, such as saving for retirement versus spending on immediate pleasures, which can lead to disagreements.

4. **Debt Management:** How couples handle debt (e.g., student loans, credit cards) can also be a source of conflict if one partner feels overwhelmed by the other's financial obligations.

5. **Lack of Communication:** Poor communication about finances often exacerbates misunderstandings and leads to unresolved issues.

Effects of Unchecked Financial Disagreements

If financial disagreements are not addressed or controlled, they can have several detrimental effects on marriages:

1. **Increased Stress:** Ongoing financial conflicts can lead to heightened stress levels for both partners, affecting their emotional well-being and overall relationship satisfaction.

2. **Erosion of Trust:** Continuous arguments about money can erode trust between partners, making them feel unsupported or misunderstood.

3. **Emotional Distance:** Persistent financial disagreements may cause partners to withdraw emotionally from each other, leading to feelings of isolation and disconnection.

4. **Divorce Risk:** Studies indicate that financial issues are among the leading causes of divorce. Couples who cannot resolve their financial differences may ultimately decide to separate.

5. **Impact on Family Dynamics:** Children may also be affected by their parents' financial disputes, which can create an unstable home environment and influence their attitudes toward money in adulthood.

Biblical Perspectives

Several Bible verses address the importance of unity and communication in marriage:

- **Ecclesiastes 4:9-10 (NIV):** "Two are better than one because they have a good return for their labour: If either of them falls down, one can help the other up."

- **Proverbs 21:20 (NIV):** "The wise store up choice food and olive oil, but fools gulp theirs down."

These verses highlight the value of partnership and wise stewardship in managing resources together.

Quotes and Sayings

Here are some relevant quotes that emphasise the importance of addressing financial disagreements:

- "Money can't buy happiness; it can only make you miserable if you don't know how to manage it." – Unknown
- "A successful marriage requires falling in love many times, always with the same person." – Mignon McLaughlin
- "Communication is key; without it, relationships fail." – Unknown

Money-related conflicts are one of the leading causes of marital strife. Differing spending habits or financial goals can create tension.

Advice

Establish a budget together and discuss financial goals openly. Consider regular financial meetings to stay aligned.

Biblical Support

Proverbs 21:20 says, "The wise store up choice food and olive oil, but fools gulp theirs down." This highlights the importance of wise financial management.

1. **Incompatibility Issue**

Incompatibility in marriages refers to the differences between partners that can lead to conflict, misunderstandings, and a lack of harmony in the relationship. These differences can manifest in various areas such as values, beliefs, interests, communication styles, and life goals. When couples are incompatible, they may struggle to connect on an emotional level or find common ground on important issues.

Types of Incompatibility

1. **Value Incompatibility:** This occurs when partners have fundamentally different beliefs about what is important in life. For example, one partner may prioritise career success while the other values family time above all else.

2. **Communication Style Incompatibility:** Differences in how individuals express themselves can lead to misunderstandings. One partner may prefer direct communication while the other uses more indirect methods.

3. **Lifestyle Incompatibility:** Variations in daily habits and lifestyle choices, such as spending habits, social activities, and health practices, can create friction.

4. **Goal Incompatibility:** Partners may have divergent aspirations regarding their future, such as differing views on having children or where to live.

Effects of Unchecked Incompatibility: If incompatibilities are not addressed or controlled, they can lead to several negative outcomes:

- **Increased Conflict:** Ongoing disagreements can escalate into frequent arguments, creating a hostile environment.

- **Emotional Distance:** Partners may begin to feel disconnected from each other due to unresolved issues.

- **Resentment**: Over time, unresolved incompatibilities can breed resentment towards one another.

- **Risk of Divorce:** Ultimately, persistent incompatibilities can lead couples to consider separation or divorce if they cannot find a way to reconcile their differences.

Examples of Incompatibility

- A couple where one partner is highly religious and the other is agnostic may face challenges in raising children with shared values.

- Partners who have vastly different financial philosophies—one being a spender and the other a saver—may experience ongoing tension over budgeting and financial planning.

Advice for Couples Entering Marriage: Biblical Perspectives

Several Bible verses offer wisdom on unity and compatibility within marriage:

- **Ephesians 4:2-3 (NIV):** "Be completely humble and gentle; be patient, bearing with one another in love. Make every effort to keep the unity of the Spirit through the bond of peace."

- **Amos 3:3 (NIV):** "Do two walk together unless they have agreed to do so?"

These verses emphasise the importance of understanding and working together as a couple.

Sayings and Quotes

"Compatibility is not about being identical; it's about finding common ground."

"In marriage, it's not about finding someone you can live with; it's about finding someone you can't live without."

"Love is not just about passion; it's also about patience and understanding."

Conclusion

In summary, incompatibility in marriages encompasses various dimensions that can significantly affect relationships if left unaddressed. Couples should strive for open communication and mutual understanding to navigate their differences effectively. Couples may discover significant differences in values, beliefs, or lifestyles that were not apparent before marriage.

Advice

Before marrying, engage in profound discussions about core values and life goals. Seek premarital counselling if necessary.

Importance of Discussing Core Values and Life Goals Before Marriage

Before entering into marriage, it is crucial for couples to engage in deep discussions about their core values and life goals. This foundational step can significantly enhance the relationship's stability and longevity. Here's a detailed exploration of why these discussions are important, how they can be approached, and some supportive resources.

Understanding Core Values

Core values are fundamental beliefs that guide an individual's behaviour and decision-making. They often include aspects such as:

- **Family**: The importance placed on family relationships and responsibilities.
- **Faith**: Spiritual beliefs and practices that shape one's worldview.
- **Career Aspirations**: Professional goals and ambitions that may affect lifestyle choices.
- **Financial Management**: Attitudes towards spending, saving, and financial planning.

Example Discussion Points

1. **Family Dynamics:** Discuss how each partner views family roles. For instance, one partner may prioritise spending time with extended family during holidays, while the other may prefer more intimate gatherings.

2. **Religious Beliefs**: If one partner is deeply religious while the other is agnostic, it's essential to discuss how this will impact their future together, especially regarding children's upbringing.

3. **Career Goals:** If one partner plans to relocate for a job opportunity, it's vital to understand how this decision affects both partners' aspirations.

Life Goals Alignment

Life goals refer to the long-term objectives individuals wish to achieve in various areas of life. These can include personal development, travel aspirations, or parenting styles.

Example Discussion Points

1. **Parenting Styles:** Couples should discuss their views on discipline, education, and lifestyle choices for their children.
2. **Lifestyle Choices:** Consideration of where to live (urban vs. rural), travel frequency, or even dietary preferences can lead to significant differences if not discussed early on.
3. **Retirement Plans:** Discussing visions for retirement, whether it involves travelling the world or settling down in a quiet community, can reveal compatibility issues.

Seeking Premarital Counselling

Premarital counselling provides couples with tools to navigate potential conflicts by facilitating open communication about sensitive topics. It often includes:

- Assessments of personality compatibility
- Discussions about conflict resolution strategies
- Explore financial management techniques

Benefits of Counselling

1. **Structured Communication:** A counsellor can help guide conversations that might otherwise be difficult.
2. **Conflict Resolution Skills:** Learning how to handle disagreements constructively can prevent future issues.
3. **Strengthening Commitment:** Engaging in counselling demonstrates a commitment to building a strong foundation for marriage.

Supportive Quotes and Verses

Here are some quotes and biblical verses that emphasise the importance of discussing core values before marriage:

Quotes

- *"A successful marriage requires falling in love many times, always with the same person."* – Mignon McLaughlin
- *"The best thing to hold onto in life is each other."* – Audrey Hepburn

Bible Verses

- *"Therefore what God has joined together, let no one separate."* – Mark 10:9 (NIV)
- *"Two are better than one because they have a good return for their labour."* – Ecclesiastes 4:9 (NIV)

Sayings for Engagement
1. "Build Your Future Together!"
2. "Talk Today for Tomorrow's Harmony."
3. "Align Your Hearts Before You Say 'I Do.'"

Conclusion

Engaging in deep discussions about core values and life goals before marriage is essential for establishing a strong partnership built on mutual understanding and respect. Seeking premarital counselling can further enhance this process by providing professional guidance tailored to each couple's unique dynamics.

Biblical Support

Amos 3:3 asks, "Do two walk together unless they have agreed to do so?" Compatibility is essential for a harmonious relationship.

4. Lack of Intimacy Issue: Understanding Lack of Intimacy in Marriages Today

Lack of intimacy in marriages today refers to the emotional, physical, and psychological disconnect that can develop between partners over time. This phenomenon is increasingly observed in contemporary relationships due to various factors such as busy lifestyles, communication barriers, and societal changes.

Emotional Intimacy

Emotional intimacy involves sharing feelings, thoughts, and experiences with one another. When couples fail to communicate openly or prioritise each other's emotional needs, they may experience a decline in intimacy. For example, a couple might become so engrossed in their careers or parenting responsibilities that they neglect to spend quality time together, leading to feelings of isolation.

Example

A husband may come home from work exhausted and choose to scroll through his phone instead of engaging with his wife about her day. Over time, this lack of engagement can create emotional distance.

Physical Intimacy

Physical intimacy encompasses the sexual relationship between partners as well as non-sexual forms of affection like hugging and kissing. A lack of physical touch can lead to feelings of rejection or inadequacy. Factors such as stress, health issues, or unresolved conflicts can contribute to reduced physical intimacy.

Example

A couple may find themselves sleeping in separate beds due to disagreements or discomforts that have not been addressed. This separation can exacerbate feelings of loneliness and disconnection.

Communication Barriers

Effective communication is key to preserving intimacy in a marriage. Misunderstandings or failure to express needs can lead to resentment and emotional withdrawal. Couples that do not practise active listening may struggle to connect on deeper levels.

Example

If one partner feels overwhelmed by household responsibilities but does not communicate this feeling effectively, they may remain unaware and continue their behaviour, leading to frustration.

Biblical Perspective

The Bible offers guidance on fostering intimacy within marriage:

- **Ephesians 5:25-28:** "Husbands, love your wives, just as Christ loved the church and gave himself up for her... In this same way, husbands ought to love their wives as their own bodies." This verse emphasises the importance of sacrificial love and mutual respect when nurturing intimacy.
- **1 Corinthians 7:3-5:** "The husband should fulfil his marital duty to his wife, and likewise the wife to her husband... Do not deprive each other except by mutual consent for a time." This passage emphasises the value of both emotional and physical connections in marriage.

Sayings and Quotes

Here are some slogans and quotes that emphasise the importance of intimacy in marriage:

- "Intimacy is not just about sex; it's about being seen and known."
- "Communication is the key that unlocks the door to intimacy."
- "In marriage, love is not just a feeling; it's an action."

Advice for Those Entering Marriage

1. **Prioritise Communication:** Make it a habit to discuss your feelings regularly.
2. **Invest Time Together:** Schedule regular date nights or activities that you both enjoy.
3. **Be Open About Needs:** Share your emotional and physical needs with your partner.
4. **Seek guidance:** Consider premarital counselling for tools for building intimacy.

By understanding these aspects of intimacy and actively working on them, couples can foster stronger connections that withstand life's challenges. Emotional or physical intimacy may wane over time due to stress or neglect, leading partners to feel disconnected.

Advice

Prioritise quality time together and maintain physical affection. Make an effort to nurture both emotional and physical intimacy regularly.

Biblical Support

1 Corinthians 7:3-4 encourages mutual fulfilment in intimacy: "The husband should fulfil his marital duty to his wife, and likewise the wife to her husband."

6. Unresolved Conflict Issue

Unresolved conflict in marriages can have profound effects on both partners and the overall health of the relationship. Understanding these effects is crucial for those considering marriage, as it can help them navigate potential challenges more effectively.

Emotional and Psychological Impact

Unresolved conflicts often lead to emotional distress for both partners. This can manifest as:

- **Increased Stress:** Constant disagreements can create a stressful environment, leading to anxiety and depression.
- **Resentment**: Over time, unresolved issues can breed resentment, making it difficult for couples to communicate openly.
- **Isolation**: Partners may feel isolated from each other, leading to emotional distance and a breakdown in intimacy.

Example

For instance, a couple that frequently argues about finances without reaching a resolution may find that their financial stress exacerbates other areas of their relationship, leading to further conflict over seemingly unrelated issues.

Communication Breakdown

Effective communication is essential for a healthy marriage. Unresolved conflicts often result in:

- **Poor Communication Skills:** Couples may resort to negative communication patterns such as yelling or stonewalling instead of constructive dialogue.
- **Avoidance**: Partners might avoid discussing important topics altogether, which can prevent resolution and understanding.

Example

A couple that avoids discussing their differing views on parenting may find themselves at odds when faced with real-life situations involving their children, leading to further disputes.

Long-term Relationship Consequences

The long-term consequences of unresolved conflict can be severe:

- **Divorce Rates:** Studies indicate that couples who do not resolve conflicts are at a higher risk for divorce. According to the American Psychological Association, nearly 40% to 50% of married couples in the United States end up divorcing.

- **Impact on Children:** Children raised in homes with unresolved conflict may experience emotional and behavioural issues. They may also struggle with relationships later in life due to the learnt behaviours they acquired from their parents.

Example

Children witnessing frequent arguments between their parents may develop anxiety or adopt similar conflict styles in their future relationships.

Biblical Perspective

From a biblical standpoint, many verses emphasise the importance of resolving conflicts and maintaining harmony in marriage.

- **Ephesians 4:26-27 (NIV):** "In your anger do not sin; do not let the sun go down while you are still angry, and do not give the devil a foothold."

- **Colossians 3:13 (NIV):** "Bear with each other and forgive one another if any of you has a grievance against someone. Forgive as the Lord forgave you."

These verses highlight the importance of addressing issues promptly and fostering forgiveness within marital relationships.

Advice for Those Entering Marriage

For individuals preparing for marriage, consider these guiding principles:

1. **Open Communication:** Establish an environment where both partners feel safe expressing their thoughts and feelings.

2. **Conflict Resolution Skills:** Learn techniques for resolving disputes amicably before they escalate.

3. **Seek Guidance:** Consider premarital counselling to address potential areas of conflict proactively.

Helpful sayings and Quotes

Here are some slogans and quotes that encapsulate the importance of resolving conflicts in marriage:

- *"Communication is key; don't let silence build walls."*
- *"Resolve today's conflicts before they become tomorrow's regrets."*
- *"A strong marriage requires two people who choose to love each other*

even on days when they struggle."

Conclusion

In summary, unresolved conflict in marriages today leads to significant emotional distress, communication breakdowns, and long-term relational consequences. By understanding these effects and applying biblical wisdom alongside practical advice, individuals entering marriage can better prepare themselves for a healthy partnership. Avoiding conflict or failing to resolve disagreements can lead to bitterness over time.

Advice

Address conflicts promptly using healthy conflict resolution techniques such as active listening and compromise.

Biblical Support

Ephesians 4:26 advises, "In your anger do not sin; do not let the sun go down while you are still angry." This underscores the importance of resolving issues quickly.

External Influences Issue

Marriages today face numerous challenges, many of which stem from external influences. These influences can significantly impact the dynamics of a relationship, leading to misunderstandings, conflicts, and even dissolution. Below, we will explore some of these external factors in detail.

1. Social Media and Technology

Social media platforms and communication technologies have transformed how couples interact with each other and the world. While they can enhance communication, they also introduce risks such as:

- **Comparison**: Couples may compare their relationships to idealised portrayals on social media, which leads to dissatisfaction.
- **Infidelity**: The anonymity and accessibility of online interactions can lead to emotional or physical infidelity.
- **Distraction**: Excessive use of devices can detract from quality time spent together.

Example

A study published in the Journal of Marriage and Family found that increased social media usage correlates with higher rates of marital dissatisfaction.

2. Economic Pressures

Financial stress is a significant external influence on marriages. Economic downturns, job loss, or financial instability can create tension between partners.

- **Conflict over finances:** Disagreements about spending habits or financial priorities can lead to arguments.

- **Stress**: Financial strain often leads to increased stress levels, which can affect communication and intimacy.

Example

According to a report by the American Psychological Association, couples who experience financial stress are more likely to report lower relationship satisfaction.

3. Cultural Expectations

Cultural norms and societal expectations can place undue pressure on marriages. This includes:

- **Gender Roles:** Traditional expectations about gender roles may create conflict if partners feel constrained by them.
- **Family Expectations:** Pressure from family members regarding decisions such as child-rearing or career choices can lead to disagreements.

Example

In many cultures, there is an expectation for couples to have children soon after marriage. This pressure can cause strain if one partner is not ready for parenthood.

4. Peer Influence

Friends and peer groups play a crucial role in shaping attitudes toward marriage. Negative influences from peers who view marriage as disposable can undermine commitment.

- **Normalisation of Divorce:** If friends frequently discuss divorce or separation casually, it may lead individuals to view their own marriages as less permanent.
- **Encouragement of Infidelity:** Friends who engage in extramarital affairs may inadvertently encourage similar behaviours in others.

Example

Research indicates that individuals whose friends have divorced are more likely to consider divorcing themselves due to the perceived normalisation of the act.

Biblical Guidance

The Bible offers wisdom on maintaining strong marriages amidst external pressures:

CHAPTER 9: Factors Contributing to Marital Failure.

- **Ephesians 4:2-3 (NIV):** "Be completely humble and gentle; be patient, bearing with one another in love. Make every effort to keep the unity of the Spirit through the bond of peace."

This verse emphasises the importance of patience and unity when overcoming challenges together.

Quotes for Reflection

Here are some quotes that provide insight into maintaining a healthy marriage:
- *"A successful marriage requires falling in love many times, always with the same person."* – Mignon McLaughlin
- *"The best thing to hold onto in life is each other."* – Audrey Hepburn

Sayings for Encouragement

Consider these slogans as reminders for those entering marriage:
- "Together through thick and thin."
- "Love conquers all challenges."

In conclusion, external influences such as social media, economic pressures, cultural expectations, and peer influence significantly impact marriages today. Recognising these factors allows couples to proactively address potential issues while drawing strength from biblical teachings and supportive quotes.

Family members or friends may exert undue influence on a couple's decisions or relationship dynamics.

Advice

Establish boundaries with external parties regarding involvement in your marriage decisions while maintaining respectful relationships with family and friends.

Biblical Support

Mark 10:9 states, "Therefore what God has joined together, let no one separate." Protecting your marriage from outside influences is crucial for its health.

Neglecting Each Other

Neglect in marriages can lead to significant emotional and relational deterioration. This phenomenon is increasingly observed in contemporary relationships, where busy lifestyles, digital distractions, and shifting societal norms contribute to a lack of attention and care between partners.

Causes of Neglect in Marriage

1. **Busy Lifestyles:** Many couples today juggle demanding careers, parenting responsibilities, and social obligations. This often leaves little time for

meaningful interactions with each other. The prioritisation of work or external commitments over a marital relationship can create a sense of distance.

2. **Digital Distractions:** The prevalence of smartphones and social media can detract from face-to-face communication. Couples may find themselves physically present but emotionally absent due to their engagement with devices rather than with each other.

3. **Lack of Communication:** Effective communication is crucial for any relationship. When couples fail to express their feelings, needs, or concerns, misunderstandings can arise, leading to feelings of neglect or resentment.

4. **Unrealistic Expectations:** Some individuals enter marriage with idealised notions about love and partnership that do not align with reality. When these expectations are not met, disappointment can lead to emotional withdrawal.

5. **Stress and Mental Health Issues:** External pressures such as financial stress or mental health challenges can cause individuals to withdraw emotionally from their partners as they struggle to cope with their issues.

Consequences of Neglect

1. **Emotional Distance:** Partners may feel more like roommates than spouses, leading to loneliness within the relationship.

2. **Increased Conflict:** Unresolved issues stemming from neglect can escalate into arguments or resentment.

3. **Infidelity**: Emotional neglect may drive one partner to seek validation or connection outside the marriage.

4. **Divorce**: In extreme cases, prolonged neglect can lead couples to consider separation as a viable solution.

How to Stop Neglect

- **Prioritise Quality Time:** Couples should intentionally set aside time for each other without distractions. Regular date nights or shared activities can help rekindle intimacy and connection.

- **Improve Communication Skills:** Engaging in open dialogues about feelings and expectations fosters understanding and reduces misunderstandings.

- **Seek Professional Help:** Marriage counselling can provide tools for better communication and conflict resolution strategies.

- **Set Realistic Expectations:** Understanding that no marriage is perfect helps couples navigate challenges without undue disappointment.

- **Practice Gratitude and Appreciation:** Regularly expressing gratitude for one another reinforces positive feelings and strengthens the bond between partners.

CHAPTER 9: Factors Contributing to Marital Failure.

Advice for Those Entering Marriage

Couples should engage in premarital counselling to discuss potential challenges they may face.

Establishing traditions or rituals that promote togetherness (e.g., weekly family meetings) can help maintain connection over time.

Bible Verses

- **Ephesians 4:2-3:** "Be completely humble and gentle; be patient, bearing with one another in love. Make every effort to keep the unity of the Spirit through the bond of peace."
- **1 Corinthians 13:4-7:** "Love is patient, love is kind... It always protects, always trusts, always hopes, always perseveres."

Popular Sayings

"Together we thrive; apart we survive."

"Communication is key; let's unlock our hearts."

Quotes

- "The best thing to hold onto in life is each other." – Audrey Hepburn
- "A successful marriage requires falling in love many times, always with the same person." – Mignon McLaughlin

By recognising the signs of neglect early on and actively working towards maintaining a healthy relationship dynamic through communication and quality time together, couples can build a strong foundation that withstands life's challenges.

Busy schedules can lead couples to neglect spending quality time together or appreciating one another's contributions.

Advice

Make intentional efforts to prioritise each other amidst busy lives—schedule regular date nights or weekend getaways when possible.

Biblical Support

Ecclesiastes 4:9-10 states that "Two are better than one... If either of them falls down, one can help the other up." Supporting each other is vital for a strong partnership.

Unrealistic Expectations in Marriage

Unrealistic expectations can destroy marriages today by creating dissatisfaction, resentment, and conflict between partners. These expectations often stem from societal influences, personal experiences, and media portrayals of relationships that do not accurately reflect the complexities of real-life partnerships.

Understanding Unrealistic Expectations

Unrealistic expectations refer to beliefs or assumptions about marriage that are not grounded in reality. They can include ideas such as:

- **The belief that love alone is enough:** Many people enter marriage thinking that love will solve all problems. However, love must be accompanied by commitment, communication, and effort.

- **Expecting a partner to fulfil all emotional needs:** Some individuals expect their spouse to be their sole source of happiness and support, which places undue pressure on the relationship.

- **Idealised views of romance:** media often portrays relationships as perfect and devoid of conflict. This can lead couples to believe that they should never argue or face challenges.

Causes of Unrealistic Expectations

Several factors contribute to the formation of unrealistic expectations in marriages:

1. **Cultural Influences:** Movies, television shows, and social media often depict idealised versions of relationships where conflicts are resolved quickly and happily ever after is guaranteed.

2. **Personal Background:** Individuals may carry over expectations from their family dynamics or previous relationships without recognising how those experiences shape their views on marriage.

3. **Lack of Communication:** Couples may enter marriage without discussing their expectations openly, leading to misunderstandings once they encounter real-life challenges.

4. **Fear of Vulnerability:** Some individuals may avoid discussing their fears or insecurities about marriage, leading them to create unrealistic standards for themselves and their partners.

How to Prevent Unrealistic Expectation

To avoid unrealistic expectations in marriage, couples can take several proactive steps:

1. **Open Communication:** Regularly discussing feelings, needs, and concerns helps build understanding and reduces misunderstandings.

2. **Setting Realistic Goals:** Couples should work together to establish achievable goals for their relationship rather than relying on idealised notions of what marriage should be like.

CHAPTER 9: Factors Contributing to Marital Failure.

3. **Embracing Imperfection:** Accepting that both partners will have flaws allows for a more compassionate approach to each other's shortcomings.
4. **Seeking Professional Guidance:** Couples therapy can provide tools for better communication and help address underlying issues contributing to unrealistic expectations.

Examples and Advice: Biblical Perspective

The Bible offers wisdom regarding relationships that emphasises love, patience, and understanding:

- "Love is patient; love is kind; it does not envy; it does not boast; it is not proud." (1 Corinthians 13:4)
- "Therefore what God has joined together, let no one separate." (Mark 10:9)

Sayings

"Real Love Requires Real Work."

"Expectations Should Be Discussed, Not Assumed."

Quotes

- *"A successful marriage requires falling in love many times, always with the same person." — Mignon McLaughlin*
- *"Marriage is not about finding someone you can live with; it's about finding someone you can't live without." — Rafael Ortiz*

By addressing unrealistic expectations through open dialogue and mutual understanding, couples can create healthier relationships built on realistic foundations rather than idealised fantasies.

Expecting perfection from one's partner can lead to disappointment when reality does not meet those expectations.

Advice

Recognise that no one is perfect; embrace each other's flaws as part of what makes you unique as individuals and as a couple.

Biblical Support

- **Romans 15:7 encourages acceptance:** "Accept one another then just as Christ accepted you..." Acceptance fosters love rather than disappointment.

Infidelity in Marriage

Infidelity, commonly understood as a breach of trust through romantic or sexual relationships outside of a committed partnership, has profound implications for marriages today. It can lead to emotional pain, loss of trust, and ultimately the dissolution of relationships.

Infidelity typically involves one partner engaging in an intimate relationship with someone outside the marriage. This can manifest in various forms, including physical affairs, emotional affairs, or even online interactions that compromise the exclusivity expected in a marital relationship. The impact of infidelity is often devastating, leading to feelings of betrayal and abandonment.

Causes of Infidelity

Several factors contribute to infidelity in modern marriages:

1. **Emotional Disconnect:** Many couples experience a decline in emotional intimacy over time. When partners feel neglected or unappreciated, they may seek validation elsewhere.

2. **Lack of Communication:** Poor communication can lead to misunderstandings and unresolved conflicts, creating an environment where one partner might look outside the marriage for connection.

3. **Opportunity**: Increased social interactions through work or social media can provide more opportunities for infidelity to occur.

4. **Dissatisfaction with Marriage:** If one or both partners are unhappy with their relationship, whether due to unmet needs or personal issues, they may be more likely to cheat.

5. **Cultural Influences:** Societal norms that downplay the seriousness of commitment can also contribute to infidelity.

Consequences of Infidelity

The consequences of infidelity are severe and multilayered:

- **Emotional Pain:** The betrayed partner often experiences intense feelings of hurt, anger, and disappointment.

- **Trust Issues:** Rebuilding trust after infidelity is challenging and requires significant effort from both partners.

- **Family Impact:** Children may suffer emotionally when parents go through separation or divorce due to infidelity.

- **Financial Strain:** Divorce proceedings can be costly and financially draining.

- **Infection and health issues?**

Finding solutions to Infidelity in Marriage

Addressing infidelity requires commitment from both partners:

1. **Open Communication:** Honest discussions about feelings and expectations can help rebuild trust.

2. **Counselling**: Professional therapy can provide tools for healing and rebuilding the relationship.
3. **Re-establishing Intimacy:** Couples should work on reconnecting emotionally and physically to strengthen their bond.
4. **Setting Boundaries:** Establishing clear boundaries regarding interactions with others can help prevent future issues.
5. **Forgiveness and Healing:** Both partners must engage in a process of forgiveness if they wish to move forward together.

Advice for Those Entering Marriage

For individuals preparing for marriage, it's essential to understand the importance of commitment and communication:

- "Love is patient; love is kind." (1 Corinthians 13:4) - This verse emphasises the need for patience and kindness within a marriage.
- "What therefore God has joined together, let not man separate." (Mark 10:9) - This highlights the sanctity of marriage vows.
- Sayings such as "Commitment is key" remind couples that dedication is crucial for a lasting relationship.
- Quotes like "A successful marriage requires falling in love many times, always with the same person" encourage couples to continually nurture their love for each other.

In conclusion, while infidelity poses significant challenges to marriages today, understanding its causes and consequences allows couples to take proactive steps toward building stronger relationships based on trust and communication. Infidelity can shatter trust between partners and often leads directly to divorce if not addressed properly.

Advice

Commitment must be reinforced through loyalty; establish clear boundaries with others outside the marriage that respect this commitment.

Biblical Support

Hebrews 13:4 warns against adultery: "Marriage should be honored by all... God will judge the adulterer..." Faithfulness is essential for marital integrity.

11. Lack of Shared Goals in Marriage

Lack of shared goals can significantly undermine the foundation of a marriage, leading to misunderstandings, resentment, and ultimately, separation.

In the context of marriage, shared goals refer to mutual aspirations and objectives that both partners agree upon and work towards together. These can include financial goals, family planning, career aspirations, lifestyle choices, and personal growth. When couples lack these shared goals, they may find themselves drifting apart as their individual priorities take precedence over the partnership.

Causes of Lack of Shared Goals

1. **Individualism:** In contemporary society, there is a strong emphasis on individualism. Partners may prioritise personal ambitions over collective ones.

2. **Communication Breakdown:** Effective communication is crucial for establishing shared goals. Couples who do not engage in open discussions about their desires and expectations may fail to align their visions for the future.

3. **Life Changes:** Major life events such as job changes, relocation, or having children can shift priorities unexpectedly. If couples do not adapt their goals accordingly through discussion and compromise, they may find themselves on divergent paths.

4. **Cultural Influences:** Societal norms and cultural backgrounds can influence how couples perceive relationships and goal-setting. Some cultures emphasise communal living and shared responsibilities more than others.

Consequences of Lack of Shared Goals

Emotional Distance: Without common objectives to rally around, partners may feel isolated in their pursuits, leading to emotional detachment.

- **Conflict:** Differing priorities can lead to disagreements over finances, parenting styles, or lifestyle choices.

- **Diminished Intimacy:** The absence of shared experiences related to common goals can reduce intimacy in a relationship.

- **Increased Risk of Divorce:** Studies indicate that couples who do not share significant life goals are at a higher risk for divorce due to unresolved conflicts and dissatisfaction.

Pathways to Re-establish Shared Goals

- **Open Communication:** Regularly discussing aspirations helps ensure both partners are aware of each other's desires and can work towards aligning them.

- **Setting Joint Objectives:** Couples should actively create joint goals that encompass both partners' interests. This could involve financial planning or setting timelines for family milestones.

- **Flexibility and Adaptation:** Life circumstances change; being willing to revisit and revise shared goals is essential for maintaining alignment in a marriage.

CHAPTER 9: Factors Contributing to Marital Failure.

- **Counselling or Workshops:** Engaging with a professional counsellor or attending workshops focused on relationship building can provide tools for effective communication and goal-setting.

Examples

A couple might start with individual career aspirations but later decide together that they want to prioritise starting a family within five years.

Another example could be two partners agreeing on saving for a home together rather than pursuing separate financial investments without consulting each other.

Biblical Perspective

The Bible emphasises unity in marriage:
- "Therefore what God has joined together, let no one separate." (Mark 10:9)
- "Two are better than one because they have a good return for their labor" (Ecclesiastes 4:9)

These verses highlight the importance of partnership and working towards common objectives as foundational elements in marriage.

Advice for Those Entering Marriage
- "A successful marriage requires falling in love many times, always with the same person." – Mignon McLaughlin
- "Love is not just about finding the right person but creating the right relationship." – Unknown
- "Together we can do so much." – Helen Keller

These quotes remind prospective couples that love involves continuous effort toward mutual understanding and shared dreams.

In conclusion, addressing the lack of shared goals through open communication and mutual commitment is vital for sustaining healthy marriages today. Couples who do not share common life goals may drift apart over time as they pursue different paths.

Advice

Discuss long-term aspirations early on. Whether related to career ambitions, family planning, or spiritual growth, and work towards shared objectives.

Biblical Support

Philippians 2:2 encourages unity in purpose: "Then make my joy complete by being like-minded..." Working towards common goals strengthens bonds.

12. Failure To Grow Together in Marriage

Failure to grow together refers to the inability of partners in a marriage to evolve and develop alongside each other, which can lead to significant emotional distance, misunderstandings, and ultimately, the breakdown of the relationship. This phenomenon is increasingly observed in modern marriages due to various societal and personal factors.

In essence, growing together means that both partners are committed to mutual development emotionally, intellectually, spiritually, and socially. When couples fail to engage in this growth process, they may find themselves drifting apart. This can manifest as a lack of shared interests, diminished communication, or differing life goals.

Causes of Failure to Grow Together

- **Lack of Communication:** Effective communication is crucial for understanding each other's needs and aspirations. When couples do not communicate openly about their feelings or future plans, misunderstandings can arise.

- **Individualism**: In contemporary society, there is a strong emphasis on individual achievement and personal fulfilment. While personal growth is important, an excessive focus on individual goals can lead couples to neglect their shared journey.

- **Life Changes:** Major life transitions such as having children, career changes, or moving can create stress that diverts attention away from nurturing the marital relationship.

- **Technological Distractions:** The rise of digital communication has altered how couples interact. Excessive screen time can detract from meaningful face-to-face interactions.

- **Unresolved Conflicts:** Ongoing disagreements that are not addressed can create resentment and emotional distance between partners.

Consequences of Not Growing Together

When couples fail to grow together:

- They may experience increased conflict due to unmet expectations.
- Emotional intimacy may decline as partners feel less connected.
- Couples might begin leading separate lives with little shared experience or understanding.
- The likelihood of infidelity or separation increases as one or both partners seek fulfilment outside the marriage.

Couples Can Grow Together by Developing:

- **Open Communication:** Regularly discussing feelings, aspirations, and concerns helps maintain connection and understanding.

- **Shared Goals:** Setting mutual goals, such as those related to finances, family planning, or personal development, to build a culture of teamwork and unity.
- **Quality Time Together:** Prioritising time spent together without distractions allows couples to reconnect and strengthen their bond.
- **Counselling:** Seeking professional help can provide tools for better communication and conflict resolution.
- **Spiritual Growth:** Engaging in spiritual practices together (such as prayer or attending religious services) can enhance emotional intimacy and shared values.

Examples & Inspirational Quotes

- A couple might decide to take a class together (e.g., cooking or dancing) as a way to bond over new experiences.
- A quote by C.S. Lewis states, "Love is not an affectionate feeling but a steady wish for the loved person's ultimate good as far as it can be obtained." This emphasises the importance of prioritising each other's growth within the marriage.

Biblical Perspective

The Bible offers guidance on relationships that emphasise unity and growth:

- Ecclesiastes 4:9-10 (NIV) states, "Two are better than one because they have a good return for their labour; if either of them falls down, one can help the other up." This verse highlights the importance of partnership in overcoming challenges together.
- Ephesians 4:2-3 (NIV) encourages humility and patience in relationships: "Be completely humble and gentle; be patient, bearing with one another in love."

As individuals evolve over time due to experiences or personal growth pursuits (education/career), couples may find themselves growing apart instead of together.

Advice

Encourage each other's growth journeys while also finding ways you can grow together—through shared activities like classes or hobbies.

Biblical Support

Colossians 3:14 emphasises love as a unifying force that binds people together during times of change: "And over all these virtues put on love..."

Conclusion

Awareness of these common pitfalls – poor communication, lack of trust, financial disagreements, incompatibility, lack of intimacy, unresolved conflict, external influences, neglecting each other, unrealistic expectations, infidelity, and lack of shared goals – combined with proactive steps informed by biblical teachings, allows new couples to build strong foundations for lasting marriages filled with love and unity.

CHAPTER 10: UNDERSTANDING DIVORCE IN THE CONTEXT OF BIBLICAL TEACHINGS

The Bible presents a comprehensive view of marriage, emphasising its sanctity and the divine intentions behind it. In Matthew 19:6, Jesus states, "So they are no longer two but one flesh. Therefore what God has joined together, let no one separate." This verse underscores the belief that marriage is ordained by God and should be treated with utmost seriousness. However, the Bible also addresses the issue of divorce and provides guidance on when it may be permissible.

Biblical Grounds for Divorce

- **1. Adultery** One of the primary grounds for divorce mentioned in the Bible is adultery. In Matthew 19:9, Jesus says, "I tell you that anyone who divorces his wife, except for sexual immorality, and marries another woman commits adultery." This indicates that infidelity breaks the covenant of marriage and provides a legitimate reason for divorce.

- **2. Abandonment** The Apostle Paul addresses abandonment in 1 Corinthians 7:15: "But if the unbeliever leaves, let it be so. The brother or sister is not bound in such circumstances; God has called us to live in peace." This passage suggests that if an unbelieving spouse chooses to leave the marriage, the believing spouse is not obligated to remain bound to that relationship.

- **3. Severe Abuse or Neglect** While not explicitly stated as a ground for divorce in scripture, many theologians interpret biblical principles regarding love and respect (Ephesians 5:25-28) to imply that severe abuse or neglect could justify separation or divorce. A marriage characterised by physical or emotional abuse contradicts the biblical call to love and protect each other.

Remedies for Offenses Leading to Divorce

While divorce may be permitted under certain circumstances according to biblical teachings, there are also remedies and paths toward reconciliation:

1. **Repentance and Forgiveness** The Bible emphasises forgiveness as a crucial aspect of relationships. In Matthew 6:14-15, Jesus teaches about forgiveness: "For if you forgive other people when they sin against you, your heavenly Father will also forgive you. But if you do not forgive others their sins, your Father will not forgive your sins." Couples facing issues such as infidelity can seek repentance and work towards rebuilding trust through forgiveness.

2. **Counselling and Mediation** Seeking counsel from church leaders or professional counsellors can provide support during difficult times. Proverbs 15:22 states, "Plans fail for lack of counsel, but with many advisers they succeed." Engaging in counselling can help couples address

underlying issues and potentially restore their relationship.

3. **Prayer and Spiritual Guidance** Prayer plays a vital role in seeking divine intervention for healing within a marriage. Philippians 4:6-7 encourages believers to present their requests to God through prayer: "Do not be anxious about anything...and the peace of God...will guard your hearts and your minds." Couples can pray together for guidance and strength during challenging times.

4. **Reconciliation Efforts** If both partners are willing to work on their relationship after an offence such as adultery or abandonment, reconciliation efforts should be made. Galatians 6:1 advises believers to restore those caught in sin gently while being mindful of their own vulnerabilities.

Conclusion

In summary, while the Bible upholds marriage as a sacred union ordained by God, stating that "what God has joined together" should not be separated, it also acknowledges specific circumstances under which divorce may occur, primarily adultery and abandonment. However, before resorting to During divorce, couples are encouraged to pursue repentance, forgiveness, counselling, prayerful consideration, and reconciliation efforts as potential remedies for offences leading to marital strife.

CHAPTER 11: THE IMPORTANCE OF CHOOSING THE RIGHT PARTNER

Choosing the right partner is a critical decision that can significantly influence an individual's life. The Bible emphasises the importance of this choice, highlighting various aspects that should be considered.

Biblical Support for Choosing Wisely

1. **Proverbs 18:22** – "He who finds a wife finds what is good and receives favour from the Lord." This verse underscores that finding a good partner is not just about personal satisfaction but also about receiving divine favour. It implies that a wise choice in a partner can lead to blessings.

2. **2 Corinthians 6:14** – "Do not be unequally yoked with unbelievers. For what partnership has righteousness with lawlessness? Or what fellowship has light with darkness?" This passage warns against forming partnerships with those who do not share similar values or beliefs, as it can lead to conflict and discord.

3. **Proverbs 31:10-31** - This passage describes the qualities of a virtuous woman, emphasising traits such as strength, wisdom, and kindness. It suggests that choosing a partner with these attributes can lead to a fulfilling and supportive relationship.

The Impact of a Good or Bad Marriage

The quality of one's marriage can have profound effects on emotional, spiritual, and physical well-being.

Positive Impacts of a Good Marriage

1. **Ecclesiastes 4:9-12** – "Two are better than one because they have a good return for their labour... If either of them falls down, one can help the other up." A strong marriage provides support and companionship, enhancing productivity and emotional resilience.

2. **Ephesians 5:25-28** – "Husbands, love your wives, just as Christ loved the church and gave himself up for her..." This passage illustrates how mutual love and respect in marriage reflect Christ's love for humanity, leading to spiritual growth and fulfilment.

Negative Impacts of a Bad Marriage

- **Proverbs 21:9** – "Better to live on a corner of the roof than share a house with a quarrelsome wife." This verse highlights the stress and unhappiness that can arise from conflict within marriage.

- **Malachi 2:16** – "For I hate divorce," says the Lord God of Israel... This indicates that broken marriages are not only painful but also displeasing to God, suggesting long-term spiritual consequences for individuals involved in unhealthy relationships.

The Role of God in Relationship Decisions

God plays an essential role in guiding individuals through their relationship choices.

Seeking Divine Guidance

- **James 1:5** – "If any of you lacks wisdom, let him ask of God..." This verse encourages believers to seek God's guidance when making decisions, including those related to relationships.

- **Psalm 37:4** – "Delight yourself in the Lord, and he will give you the desires of your heart." When individuals prioritise their relationship with God, they align their desires with His will, which can lead to better choices in partners.

- **Proverbs 3:5-6** – "Trust in the Lord with all your heart... In all your ways acknowledge him, and he will make straight your paths." Trusting God in relationship decisions ensures that individuals are led toward paths that promote healthy partnerships.

In conclusion, choosing the right partner is crucial for personal happiness and fulfilment; it significantly impacts one's life quality through both positive support systems and negative experiences, depending on the nature of the relationship. Furthermore, seeking God's guidance throughout this process is vital for making informed decisions aligned with divine principles.

CHAPTER 12: SPIRITUAL COMPATIBILITY

Why Spiritual Alignment Matters (2 Corinthians 6:14)

Spiritual alignment in relationships is a significant aspect of compatibility, particularly for those who prioritise their faith in their personal lives. The biblical reference from 2 Corinthians 6:14 states, "Do not be unequally yoked together with unbelievers. For what fellowship has righteousness with lawlessness? And what communion has light with darkness?" This verse emphasises the importance of shared beliefs and values in fostering a harmonious relationship.

Importance of Shared Beliefs

1. **Foundation of Values:** Shared spiritual beliefs often serve as a foundation for core values, guiding principles, and moral decisions within a relationship. When partners have similar beliefs, they are more likely to agree on issues such as family dynamics, financial management, and ethical considerations.

2. **Emotional Support:** A partner who shares your spiritual beliefs can provide emotional support during challenging times. This mutual understanding can foster deeper connections and resilience against external pressures.

3. **Community and Worship:** Couples who share the same faith often participate together in community activities and worship services, enhancing their bond through shared experiences and social networks.

4. **Conflict Resolution:** Similar spiritual perspectives can lead to more effective conflict resolution strategies. Partners may draw upon their shared beliefs to navigate disagreements constructively.

Identifying a Godly Partner

Identifying a godly partner involves looking for qualities that reflect spiritual maturity and alignment with one's own faith values. Here are some key characteristics to consider:

1. **Faithfulness**: A godly partner should demonstrate commitment to their faith through regular practices such as prayer, reading scripture, and attending religious services.

2. **Character Traits:** Look for traits such as kindness, patience, humility, and integrity – qualities that align with biblical teachings.

3. **Shared Goals:** Discuss long-term goals related to spirituality, family life, and personal growth to ensure alignment in vision for the future.

4. **Openness to Growth:** A willingness to grow spiritually together is essential; this includes being open to discussing faith-related topics and supporting each other's spiritual journeys.

5. **Community Involvement:** Active participation in a faith community can indicate a commitment to one's beliefs and provide opportunities for shared experiences.

Advantages and Disadvantages

Advantages

- **Stronger Bonds:** Spiritual compatibility can lead to stronger emotional bonds due to shared values and experiences.

- **Unified Parenting Approach:** Couples aligned spiritually are likely to have similar views on parenting styles, which can create consistency for children.

- **Supportive Environment:** A shared belief system creates an environment where both partners feel supported in their individual spiritual journeys.

- **Shared Purpose:** Working towards common spiritual goals can enhance the sense of purpose within the relationship.

Disadvantages

- **Limited Perspectives:** Focusing solely on spiritual compatibility may limit exposure to diverse viewpoints that could enrich the relationship.

- **Potential for Judgement:** Differences in levels of faith or practice may lead one partner to feel judged or inadequate if they do not meet the other's expectations.

- **Exclusivity Concerns:** Emphasising spiritual alignment might unintentionally exclude potential partners who possess other valuable qualities but differ in belief systems.

- **Conflict Over Beliefs:** If one partner's beliefs evolve or change significantly over time, it could create tension or conflict within the relationship.

In conclusion, while spiritual compatibility plays a crucial role in forming strong relationships based on mutual understanding and shared values, it is also essential to recognise the potential limitations that come with focussing solely on this aspect when seeking a partner.

CHAPTER 13: CHARACTER AND INTEGRITY

Importance of Good Character (Proverbs 31:10-12)

Good character is often regarded as one of the most essential qualities in a partner, particularly when considering long-term commitments such as marriage. The biblical passage from Proverbs 31:10-12 states, "Who can find a virtuous woman? For her worth is far above rubies. The heart of her husband safely trusts her, so he will have no lack of gain. She does him good and not evil all the days of her life." This scripture highlights several key aspects regarding the importance of character

Value Beyond Material Wealth

The reference to a virtuous woman being "worth far above rubies" signifies that good character transcends material wealth or physical beauty. It emphasises that true value lies in integrity, virtue, and moral strength.

Trustworthiness

The phrase "the heart of her husband safely trusts her" underscores the significance of trust in a relationship. A partner with good character creates an environment where both individuals feel secure and confident in each other's intentions and actions.

Consistency in Actions

The verse also mentions that she "does him good and not evil all the days of her life", indicating that good character is reflected through consistent actions over time. A person with integrity acts ethically and responsibly, regardless of circumstances, which contributes to a stable and nurturing relationship.

Consideration – In a world where women feel pressured and oppressed, it would be important to bring balance to this character and integrity topic.

These Bible texts particularly charge males (husbands) to be of excellent character in their marriage, therefore delineating their scriptural responsibilities:

1. **Emphasis on Love, Respect, and Honour:**

Ephesians 5:25 to 33. Possibly one of the most straightforward and thorough accusations against New Testament spouses is this one. It exhorts husbands to love their spouses with a sacrificial love fashioned like Christ's love for the church.

"Husbands, love your wives, as Christ loved the church and gave himself up for her," verse 25 says. **Obligation/character:** Such an obligation demands a selfless, altruistic love. Even in cases of self-sacrifice, a husband's character should be distinguished by a readiness to give his wife's welfare and spiritual development top priority.

Verse 28: "In the same manner, husbands need to cherish their wives as their own bodies. The person who loves his wife loves himself." Compared to the natural care one provides for their own body, this highlights the union of husband and wife by stressing their obligation/character. It implies compassion, defence, and encouragement. "For no one ever hated his flesh, but nourishes and cherishes it, just as Christ does the church," verse 29 says. Husbands are commanded to "nourish and cherish" their spouses. This relates to meeting her bodily, emotional, and spiritual needs as well as to showing her compassion and care.

Colossians 3:19 offers a succinct but strong directive about a husband's attitude to his wife.

"Husbands, love your wives, and do not be harsh with them." Verse 19 [2]
Obligation/character: This restates the directive to love and adds a particular ban against harshness or bitterness. In his contacts with his wife, a husband should be soft, patient, and kind, thereby avoiding rage or violence.
Peter 3:7, 1 Peter 3:7. This passage speaks to husbands personally, tying their spiritual lives and prayers to their treatment of their spouses.

Verse 7: "Likewise, husbands, live with your wives in an understanding way, showing honour to the woman as the weaker vessel since they are heirs with you by the grace of life so that your prayers may not be hindered."
Obligation/Character: This chapter encourages men to live "in an understanding way", therefore suggesting empathy, thoughtfulness, and communication. They are charged to show "honour" to their spouses; they honour their intrinsic dignity and equal position as "heirs with you by the grace of life". This duty calls for a virtue of respect, knowledge, and spiritual cooperation. The cited results emphasise the weight of this responsibility, as failure might affect a husband's connection with God.

Proverbs 5:18 19 Although this wisdom book encourages constancy and joy in one's wife, it does not impose demands in the same way as the writings of the New Testament.

Verses 18–19: "Let your spring be blessed, and exult in the woman of your youth, a handsome deer, a graceful doe. Let her breasts please you at all times; be inebriated continually in her affection." Fourth
Specifically with his wife, this chapter exhorts a husband to discover delight, fulfilment, and loyalty inside his marriage. It speaks to a character of satisfaction, loyalty, and love for the marriage connection.

Malachi 2:14–16 Emphasises the covenant character of marriage, this Old Testament chapter sharply condemns adultery and abuse of one's wife.

"...the Lord was witness between you and your wife, whom you have been

Chapter 13: Character and Integrity

unfaithful to, though she is your companion and covenant wife..." Verses 14–16 state that the Lord, God of Israel, condemns the man who does not love his wife but chooses to divorce her, describing this act as covering his garment with violence. Thus, guard yourselves in your spirit and avoid becoming faithless."
Character/Obligation: This chapter emphasises the husband's need for loyalty and his avoidance of "treacherously" treating his wife. It emphasises the gravity of marital relationships from God's perspective and exhorts a moral attitude that includes loyalty, dependability, and dedication.

By emphasising love, sacrifice, kindness, understanding, honour, loyalty, and protection, these texts, taken together, offer a clear Biblical foundation for the character and responsibilities required of men in a Christian marriage.

Emphasis on Faithfulness and Purity:

Stressing purity and faithfulness

Many warnings against adultery and sexual immorality found in the Bible provide men and women a clear direction on how to maintain loyalty and purity in their relationships. Important songs include Exodus 20:14, "You shall not commit adultery," which underlines the moral need of fidelity. Likewise, Matthew 5:28 underlines that even harbouring lustful ideas might be equivalent to committing adultery in one's heart; therefore, extending the idea of faithfulness beyond simple physical deeds to encompass mental and emotional integrity.

Furthermore, supporting this idea is Hebrews 13:4, which states, "Marriage should be honoured by all, and the marriage bed should be kept pure," thereby stressing that purity is not just a personal virtue but also necessary for the sanctity of marriage. These scripture examples, taken together, highlight how basic integrity is in every committed relationship, and it is not only a recommendation.

Basically, building trust and closeness between couples depends on keeping loyalty and purity. It guarantees that both people feel safe and valuable, therefore laying the basis on which good partnerships may flourish. Couples trying to honour their promises to one another find direction from a biblical viewpoint of these qualities.

Focussing on Provision and Care

"Anyone who does not provide for their relatives, and especially for their household, has denied the faith and is worse than an unbeliever," declares 1 Timothy 5:8 (NIV). This chapter emphasises people's great obligations towards their families. Taking care of one's family represents a deeper feeling of commitment, responsibility, and care than only a financial one. Good character requires these traits absolutely. Neglecting this obligation might make one less moral as they reject the basic principles connected with family support and care.

The emphasis here is on the importance of actively providing emotional and practical care for one's family. This clause covers emotional support and caring connections inside the home in addition to basic necessities. Thus, assuming this responsibility shows a dedication to one's family and helps one define their character through their behaviour.

Stress on Knowledge and Insight

Proverbs 24:3-4 (NIV) expresses, "By wisdom a house is built, and through understanding it is established; through knowledge its rooms are filled with rare and beautiful treasures." This chapter addresses the fundamental components needed to build a solid home environment. Although it tackles the overall idea of constructing a house, it especially relates to the responsibility of a husband or partner in encouraging knowledge and understanding inside a marriage.

Good character entails not just gaining knowledge but also using it in interactions. In this sense, wisdom might be defined as the capacity to make wise judgements that favour both spouses in marriage. Understanding means recognising our different needs, feelings, and points of view. Combining these attributes into their relationship dynamics helps people create an environment where love, respect, and personal development blossom.

All things considered, excellent character consists mostly in one's family's needs as well as in the search for knowledge. They show a person's dedication to developing relationships and fulfilling duties that support a positive family life.

Signs of True Integrity

Identifying true integrity in a partner requires recognising specific traits and behaviours that reflect their moral compass. Here are some signs to look for:

- **Honesty**

A person with integrity values truthfulness and transparency. They communicate openly about their thoughts, feelings, and intentions without deceit or manipulation.

- **Accountability**

Individuals who demonstrate integrity take responsibility for their actions. They acknowledge their mistakes, learn from them, and strive to make amends rather than deflect blame onto others.

- **Consistency**

Integrity is characterised by consistency between one's words and actions. A person with integrity behaves according to their principles regardless of who is watching or what situation they are in.

- **Respect for Others**

True integrity involves treating others with respect, kindness, and fairness.

This includes valuing differing opinions and showing empathy towards others' experiences.

- **Commitment to Values**

A person with strong character adheres to their core values even when faced with challenges or temptations. They prioritise ethical considerations over personal gain or convenience.

How Character Influences Marriage

Character plays a pivotal role in shaping the dynamics within a marriage. Here are several ways in which strong character influences marital relationships:

- **Foundation for**

A marriage built on mutual trust allows partners to feel secure in sharing vulnerabilities, aspirations, and fears. When both individuals possess strong character traits such as honesty and accountability, it creates an atmosphere where trust can flourish.

- **Conflict Resolution**

Couples with strong character are better equipped to handle conflicts constructively. They approach disagreements with respect for one another's perspectives while seeking solutions rather than resorting to blame or hostility.

- **Emotional Support**

Partners who exhibit good character provide emotional support during challenging times. Their reliability creates a safe space for expressing feelings without fear of judgement or ridicule.

- **Role Modelling for Future Generations**

Marriages characterised by strong moral values serve as positive role models for children or future generations. Children raised in such environments learn the importance of integrity, respect, and accountability through observation.

- **Long-Term Satisfaction**

Research indicates that marriages founded on shared values, including strong character, tend to experience higher levels of satisfaction over time. Couples who prioritise integrity often report greater happiness due to enhanced communication, mutual respect, and emotional connections.

In conclusion, the significance of character and integrity cannot be overstated when it comes to forming healthy relationships, especially marriages. By prioritising these qualities in oneself and seeking them out in potential partners, individuals can build lasting bonds rooted in trust, respect, and shared values.

CHAPTER 14: PURPOSE AND VISION ALIGNMENT

The Role of Shared Vision in a Relationship (Amos 3:3)

A shared vision is fundamental to the success and sustainability of any relationship, whether personal or professional. The biblical reference from Amos 3:3 states, "Can two walk together, except they be agreed?" This verse underscores the importance of agreement and alignment in purpose for effective collaboration and harmony. When individuals share a common vision, they are more likely to work cohesively towards their goals, creating mutual understanding and support.

Importance of Shared Vision

1. **Unity**: A shared vision creates a sense of unity among individuals. It aligns their efforts and energies towards a common goal, reducing conflicts that may arise from differing objectives.

2. **Motivation**: When individuals believe in a shared vision, they are often more motivated to contribute their best efforts. This collective motivation can lead to increased productivity and satisfaction within the relationship.

3. **Direction**: A clear vision provides direction for decision-making processes. It serves as a guiding star that helps individuals navigate challenges and make choices that are consistent with their shared goals.

4. **Resilience**: Relationships with a strong shared vision tend to be more resilient in the face of adversity. When challenges arise, partners can draw on their common purpose to overcome obstacles together.

How to Identify Alignment in Purpose

Identifying alignment in purpose requires introspection, communication, and evaluation of individual goals against the collective vision. Here are steps to effectively identify alignment:

1. **Open Communication:** Engage in honest discussions about each individual's values, aspirations, and expectations. This dialogue should encourage vulnerability and openness.

2. **Define Core Values:** Each party should articulate their core values and beliefs that drive their actions. Understanding these values can help identify areas of overlap or divergence.

3. **Set Common Goals:** Collaboratively establish specific goals that reflect the shared vision. These goals should be measurable and time-bound to facilitate tracking progress.

4. **Regular Check-Ins:** Schedule periodic evaluations to assess progress towards the shared goals. These check-ins provide an opportunity to recalibrate if necessary and ensure continued alignment.

5. **Feedback Mechanism:** Create a system for providing constructive feedback on how well each individual is contributing towards the shared vision. This encourages accountability and creates growth.

6. **Visual Representation:** Sometimes visual aids like charts or diagrams can help illustrate how individual purposes align with the collective vision, making it easier to see connections or gaps.

Challenges of Misalignment

Misalignment in purpose can lead to significant challenges within relationships:

1. **Conflict:** differing objectives can result in misunderstandings or disagreements that escalate into conflict if not addressed promptly.

2. **Decreased Motivation:** When individuals feel disconnected from the shared vision, their motivation may wane, leading to disengagement from the relationship's activities.

3. **Inefficiency:** Misalignment often leads to wasted resources – time, energy, and finances – on initiatives that do not contribute toward common goals.

4. **Loss of Trust:** Continuous misalignment can erode trust between parties, as one may feel that their needs or perspectives are being overlooked or undervalued.

5. **Emotional Strain:** The stress associated with navigating misaligned purposes can take an emotional toll on individuals involved, potentially leading to burnout or resentment over time.

6. **Stagnation:** Without a unified direction, relationships may stagnate as partners become hesitant to pursue new opportunities or innovations due to uncertainty about each other's commitment levels.

In conclusion, aligning purpose and vision is crucial for nurturing healthy relationships characterised by unity, motivation, resilience, and effective collaboration while avoiding potential pitfalls associated with misalignment, such as conflict and inefficiency.

CHAPTER 15: COMMUNICATION AND UNDERSTANDING

The Power of Effective Communication (Ephesians 4:29)

Effective communication is a cornerstone of healthy relationships, as it fosters understanding, connection, and collaboration. The biblical reference from Ephesians 4:29 states, "Let no corrupt communication proceed out of your mouth, but that which is good to the use of edifying, that it may minister grace unto the hearers." This verse emphasises the importance of speaking in ways that build others up rather than tear them down.

Importance of Effective Communication

1. **Building Trust:** Open and honest communication builds trust between individuals. When people feel heard and understood, they are more likely to share their thoughts and feelings without fear of judgement.

2. **Conflict Resolution:** Effective communication is essential for resolving conflicts. It allows individuals to express their concerns clearly and listen to each other's perspectives, facilitating a constructive dialogue.

3. **Emotional Connection:** Sharing thoughts and feelings creates emotional intimacy. When partners communicate effectively, they can connect on a deeper level, enhancing their bond.

4. **Clarity and Understanding:** Clear communication reduces misunderstandings and misinterpretations. It ensures that all parties have a shared understanding of expectations, goals, and responsibilities.

5. **Encouragement and Support:** Positive communication encourages individuals to support one another through challenges. Words of affirmation can uplift spirits and motivate individuals to persevere.

How to Assess Communication Skills

Assessing communication skills involves evaluating both verbal and non-verbal aspects of interaction. Here are steps to effectively assess these skills:

1. **Self-Reflection:** Individuals should reflect on their communication styles by considering how they express themselves verbally and non-verbally. Questions such as "Do I listen actively?" or "Am I clear in my explanations?" can guide this reflection.

2. **Feedback from Others:** Seeking feedback from trusted friends or colleagues can offer helpful observations about one's communication effectiveness. Constructive criticism can highlight areas for improvement.

3. **Active Listening Assessment:** Evaluate how well you listen during conversations. Active listening involves fully concentrating on what is being said rather than merely waiting for your turn to speak. Consider whether you ask clarifying questions or paraphrase what others say to ensure understanding.

4. **Non-Verbal Cues:** Pay attention to body language, facial expressions, eye contact, and tone of voice during interactions. Non-verbal cues often convey more meaning than words alone; assessing these can reveal underlying emotions or attitudes.

5. **Role-Playing Scenarios:** Engaging in role-playing exercises with a partner can help simulate real-life conversations where individuals can practise their communication skills in a safe environment while receiving immediate feedback.

6. **Communication Style Inventory:** Utilise tools such as personality assessments or communication style inventories (e.g., DISC assessment) that categorise different styles of communication (assertive, passive-aggressive) to gain insight into personal tendencies.

Common Issues and How to Overcome Them

Despite the importance of effective communication, several common issues may arise that hinder clear interaction:

1. Misunderstandings:

- **Issue**: Misinterpretation of messages due to ambiguous language or assumptions.

- **Solution**: Encourage clarification by asking open-ended questions like "What do you mean by that?" or summarising what was said before responding.

2. Defensiveness:

- **Issue**: Individuals may become defensive when receiving feedback or criticism.

- **Solution**: Create an environment where constructive feedback is framed positively; emphasise intentions behind comments (e.g., "I want us both to succeed").

3. Lack of Active Listening:

- **Issue**: One party may dominate conversations while the other feels unheard.

- **Solution**: Implement active listening techniques such as nodding affirmatively, maintaining eye contact, and summarising points made by the speaker before responding.

4. Emotional Barriers:

- **Issue**: Strong emotions (anger, sadness) can cloud judgement during discussions.
- **Solution**: Take breaks if emotions run high; return to the conversation when both parties feel calmer for more productive dialogue.

5. Cultural Differences:

- **Issue**: Variations in cultural backgrounds may lead to differing interpretations or expectations regarding communication styles.
- **Solution**: Cultivate cultural awareness by educating oneself about different cultures' norms around expression; approach conversations with curiosity rather than judgement.

6. Technology Miscommunication:

- **Issue**: Digital communications (texts/emails) lack non-verbal cues, leading to potential misinterpretations.
- **Solution**: Use clear language in written communications; consider following up with a phone call or video chat for sensitive topics requiring nuance.

In conclusion, effective communication plays a vital role in creating understanding within relationships by building trust, resolving conflicts constructively, enhancing emotional connections, and ensuring clarity in interactions while addressing common issues through proactive strategies aimed at overcoming barriers present in everyday exchanges.

CHAPTER 16: EMOTIONAL MATURITY AND STABILITY

Why Emotional Maturity is Key (Proverbs 14:29)

Emotional maturity refers to the ability to understand, manage, and express one's emotions effectively while also being able to empathise with others. Proverbs 14:29 states, "Whoever is slow to anger has great understanding, but he who has a hasty temper exalts folly." This verse highlights the importance of emotional regulation and patience as indicators of wisdom and maturity.

Understanding Emotional Responses

Emotionally mature individuals can recognise their emotional triggers and respond appropriately rather than react impulsively. This self-awareness allows them to navigate complex social situations without escalating conflicts or causing misunderstandings. They are more likely to engage in constructive communication, which creates healthier relationships.

Impact on Relationships

Emotional maturity is crucial for maintaining stable relationships. Individuals who exhibit emotional maturity tend to be more reliable, supportive, and understanding partners. They can handle stressors together without resorting to blame or defensiveness, which contributes to a more harmonious relationship environment.

Long-term Benefits

In the long run, emotionally mature individuals are better equipped to face life's challenges. Their ability to manage emotions leads to improved mental health outcomes, reduced anxiety levels, and greater overall life satisfaction. Thus, emotional maturity serves as a foundation for personal growth and fulfilling relationships.

How to Recognise Emotional Stability

Recognising emotional stability for oneself or others involves observing specific behaviours and traits that indicate a balanced emotional state.

Key Indicators of Emotional Stability

1. **Self-Regulation:** Emotionally stable individuals can control their impulses and reactions. They do not overreact in stressful situations but instead take time to process their feelings before responding.

2. **Resilience**: The ability to bounce back from setbacks is a hallmark of

emotional stability. Such individuals view challenges as opportunities for growth rather than insurmountable obstacles.

3. **Empathy**: An emotionally stable person demonstrates an understanding of others' feelings and perspectives. They listen actively and respond with compassion rather than judgement.
4. **Consistent Behaviour**: Stability often manifests as consistent behaviour over time; emotionally stable individuals do not frequently swing between extreme moods or attitudes.
5. **Healthy Coping Mechanisms**: Instead of resorting to unhealthy habits like substance abuse or avoidance strategies when faced with stress, emotionally stable people employ positive coping mechanisms such as exercise, mindfulness practices, or seeking support from friends.

Assessing Your Own Emotional Stability

Self-reflection is key in recognising one's own emotional stability. Journaling about your daily experiences and emotions can provide insights into patterns of behaviour that may need addressing. Additionally, seeking feedback from trusted friends or family members can offer an external perspective on one's emotional responses.

Benefits of Choosing a Mature Partner

Choosing a partner who exhibits emotional maturity brings numerous advantages that contribute positively to the relationship dynamic.

- **Enhanced Communication**

Mature partners are typically better communicators; they express their thoughts clearly and listen actively without interrupting or dismissing each other's feelings. This open line of communication reduces misunderstandings and builds intimacy.

- **Conflict Resolution Skills**

Emotionally mature individuals approach conflicts with a problem-solving mindset rather than engaging in blame games or defensiveness. They are willing to compromise and find solutions that work for both parties involved.

- **Supportive Environment**

A mature partner provides a supportive environment where both individuals feel safe expressing their vulnerabilities without fear of judgement or ridicule. This nurturing atmosphere encourages personal growth for both partners.

- **Shared Values and Goals**

Partners who demonstrate emotional maturity often share similar values regarding relationships, family dynamics, financial management, and future aspirations. This alignment helps create a unified vision for the future.

- **Greater Relationship Satisfaction**

Research indicates that relationships characterised by mutual respect, understanding, and effective communication lead to higher levels of satisfaction among partners. Choosing an emotionally mature partner significantly increases the likelihood of long-term happiness together.

In conclusion, recognising the importance of emotional maturity in oneself and potential partners can lead to healthier relationships characterised by effective communication, resilience during challenges, empathy towards each other's experiences, and overall satisfaction in partnership dynamics.

CHAPTER 17: FINANCIAL RESPONSIBILITY

Importance of Financial Stewardship (Proverbs 22:7)

Financial stewardship refers to the responsible management of financial resources, including income, expenses, savings, and investments. Proverbs 22:7 states, "The rich rules over the poor, and the borrower is the slave of the lender." This verse underscores the importance of understanding financial dynamics and the implications of debt.

Understanding Financial Stewardship

1. **Resource Management:** Financial stewardship involves making informed decisions about how to allocate resources effectively. This includes budgeting, saving for emergencies, investing for future growth, and planning for retirement. Responsible management ensures that individuals can meet their current needs while preparing for future challenges.

2. **Avoiding Debt:** The proverb highlights a critical aspect of financial stewardship: avoiding unnecessary debt. Living within one's means is essential to maintaining financial independence and stability. When individuals take on excessive debt, they may find themselves in a precarious situation where they are beholden to lenders, limiting their freedom and choices.

3. **Long-term Planning:** Effective financial stewardship requires a long-term perspective. Individuals should set financial goals that align with their values and aspirations, whether it's buying a home, funding education for children, or ensuring a comfortable retirement. A proactive approach to saving and investing can lead to greater security and peace of mind.

4. **Generosity**: Stewardship also encompasses the idea of giving back to the community or supporting charitable causes. By managing finances wisely, individuals can contribute positively to society while fulfilling their own needs.

Recognising Financial Habits

Recognising one's financial habits is crucial for achieving financial responsibility. These habits can be categorised into positive and negative behaviours that influence overall financial health.

Positive Financial Habits

1. **Budgeting:** Creating and adhering to a budget allows individuals to track income and expenses systematically. This practice helps identify areas where spending can be reduced or adjusted.

2. **Saving Regularly:** Establishing a habit of saving, whether through automatic transfers to savings accounts or setting aside a percentage of income,

can build an emergency fund that provides security during unforeseen circumstances.

3. **Investing Wisely:** Educating oneself about investment options and making informed decisions can lead to wealth accumulation over time. Diversifying investments reduces risk while maximising potential returns.

4. **Continuous Learning:** Staying informed about personal finance topics through books, courses, or seminars enhances one's ability to make sound financial decisions.

Negative Financial Habits

1. **Impulse Spending:** Making unplanned purchases without considering their impact on overall finances can lead to budget overruns and increased debt levels.

2. **Living Beyond Means:** Consistently spending more than what one earns creates unsustainable financial pressure that often results in borrowing or accumulating credit card debt.

3. **Neglecting Savings:** Failing to prioritise savings can leave individuals vulnerable in emergencies or when unexpected expenses arise.

4. **Avoidance of Financial Planning:** Ignoring the need for budgeting or long-term planning can result in missed opportunities for growth and increased stress regarding future financial stability.

Money and Marriage Challenges

Financial issues are among the leading causes of conflict in marriages; therefore, addressing money matters openly is essential for maintaining harmony in relationships.

Common Money Challenges in Marriage

1. **Differing Attitudes Toward Money:** Partners may have contrasting views on spending versus saving based on their upbringing or personal experiences with money management. These differences can lead to misunderstandings if not addressed openly.

2. **Debt Discrepancies:** One partner may enter the marriage with significant debt while another has managed their finances responsibly; this disparity can create tension as couples navigate shared responsibilities.

3. **Budgeting Conflicts:** Disagreements over how much should be allocated toward various expenses, such as housing costs versus entertainment, can lead to frustration if both partners do not agree on priorities.

4. **Financial Goals Misalignment:** Couples may have different visions regarding future goals such as homeownership, travel plans, or retirement savings, which could cause friction if not discussed early on in the relationship.

Strategies for Managing Money Challenges

1. **Open Communication:** Establishing regular discussions about finances creates transparency between partners regarding income sources, expenditures, debts, and savings goals.

2. **Joint Budgeting Sessions:** Collaboratively creating a budget allows both partners to voice their opinions on spending priorities while ensuring alignment toward shared objectives.

3. **Setting Shared Goals:** Identifying common short-term and long-term financial goals encourages teamwork within the marriage as both partners work together towards achieving these aspirations.

4. **Seeking Professional Guidance:** If conflicts persist despite efforts at communication and collaboration, consulting with a financial advisor or counsellor specialising in marital finances may provide valuable insights into resolving issues constructively.

In conclusion, understanding financial responsibility through stewardship principles is vital for individual well-being as well as relationship harmony within marriages facing monetary challenges; recognising habits, both positive and negative, and creating open dialogue around finances will ultimately contribute towards healthier partnerships built upon trust rather than tension surrounding money matters.

CHAPTER 18: FAMILY BACKGROUND AND VALUES

How Family Values Affect Marriage (Exodus 20:12)

Family values play a crucial role in shaping the dynamics of marriage. According to Exodus 20:12, which states, "Honour your father and your mother," the importance of familial respect and values is emphasised as foundational to societal structure. This commandment not only highlights the significance of honouring parents but also implies that the values instilled by them can significantly influence marital relationships.

1. **Foundation of Values:** The family unit is often where individuals first learn about love, respect, communication, and conflict resolution. These early lessons shape expectations and behaviours in adult relationships. For instance, if a person grew up in a household where open communication was encouraged, they are likely to carry this value into their marriage.

2. **Expectations from Partners:** Family values can dictate what individuals expect from their partners. For example, traditional families may emphasise gender roles that influence how spouses view responsibilities within the marriage. A person raised in a family that prioritises egalitarian principles may seek a partnership based on shared responsibilities rather than traditional roles.

3. **Conflict Resolution:** The way conflicts are handled in one's family can affect how an individual approaches disagreements in marriage. Families that model healthy conflict resolution strategies tend to produce adults who are better equipped to navigate disputes constructively.

4. **Cultural Heritage:** Cultural backgrounds significantly impact family values and consequently affect marriages. Different cultures have varying beliefs about marriage roles, expectations regarding children, and even financial management within a relationship.

Understanding Cultural and Traditional Influences

Cultural influences extend beyond individual families to encompass broader societal norms that shape perceptions of marriage.

1. **Cultural Norms:** Each culture has its own set of traditions and practices surrounding marriage that can dictate everything from courtship rituals to post-marital living arrangements. For example, some cultures may place a strong emphasis on arranged marriages, while others prioritise romantic love as the basis for marriage.

2. **Tradition vs Modernity:** In many societies today, there is often tension between traditional values and modern perspectives on marriage. Individuals may struggle with balancing familial expectations with personal desires for autonomy or equality within their relationships.

3. **Religious Beliefs:** Religion often plays a significant role in shaping family values related to marriage. Many religious teachings provide guidelines on marital conduct, roles within the relationship, and even divorce, which can heavily influence how individuals approach their marriages.

Handling Differences Wisely

Navigating differences arising from diverse family backgrounds requires wisdom and understanding:

1. **Open Communication:** Couples should engage in open discussions about their respective family backgrounds and values before entering into marriage or during its early stages. This dialogue helps clarify expectations and identify potential areas of conflict.

2. **Empathy and Respect:** It is essential for partners to approach each other's backgrounds with empathy and respect. Understanding why certain values are important to one's partner can create deeper connections and reduce friction over differing viewpoints.

3. **Compromise:** Healthy marriages often require compromise when it comes to differing family values or cultural practices. Couples should work together to find solutions that honour both partners' backgrounds while creating new traditions unique to their union.

4. **Seeking Guidance:** Sometimes, couples may benefit from seeking guidance from counsellors or mentors who understand the complexities of blending different family backgrounds into one cohesive partnership.

In conclusion, family background and values have a profound impact on marriages through established norms surrounding communication, conflict resolution, expectations from partners, cultural influences, and religious beliefs. By understanding these factors and handling differences wisely through open communication, empathy, compromise, and guidance when necessary, couples can build strong foundations for lasting relationships.

CHAPTER 19: MUTUAL RESPECT AND LOVE

The Role of Love and Respect (Ephesians 5:33)

In Ephesians 5:33, the Apostle Paul writes, "Each one of you also must love his wife as he loves himself, and the wife must respect her husband." This verse encapsulates the dual pillars of a healthy marriage: love and respect.

Importance of Love

Love serves as the emotional foundation of a relationship. It creates intimacy, connection, and a sense of belonging between partners. When love is present in a marriage, it encourages:

- **Emotional Support:** Partners who love each other provide comfort during difficult times.
- **Affection**: Expressions of love through physical touch, kind words, and thoughtful gestures strengthen bonds.
- **Commitment**: A loving relationship promotes loyalty and dedication to one another.

Importance of Respect

Respect is equally vital in maintaining a balanced partnership. It involves recognising each other's worth and treating one another with dignity. Key aspects include:

- **Valuing Opinions:** Each partner should feel that their thoughts and feelings are important.
- **Acknowledging Boundaries:** Respecting personal space and individual needs is crucial for emotional well-being.
- **Support for Growth:** Encouraging each other's personal development demonstrates respect for individual aspirations.

Together, love and respect create an environment where both partners can thrive emotionally and psychologically.

How to Assess Respect in a Relationship

Assessing respect within a relationship requires careful observation of behaviours and interactions between partners. Here are some indicators to consider:

Communication Style

- **Active Listening:** Are both partners genuinely listening to each other without interrupting?
- **Constructive Feedback:** Do they provide feedback that is supportive rather than critical?

Decision-Making

- **Inclusivity**: Are both partners involved in making decisions that affect their lives together?
- **Consideration of Needs:** Is there an effort to consider each other's preferences when making choices?

Conflict Resolution

- **Healthy Disagreements:** Do disagreements lead to constructive discussions rather than insults or dismissiveness?
- **Apologies and Forgiveness:** Are partners willing to apologise when wrong and forgive each other's mistakes?

Supportive Actions

- **Encouragement**: Do partners encourage each other's goals and ambitions?
- **Acts of Kindness:** Are there regular expressions of kindness that demonstrate thoughtfulness?

By evaluating these aspects, couples can gain insight into the level of respect present in their relationship.

Red Flags to Watch Out For

While assessing respect in a relationship, it is essential to be vigilant for red flags that may indicate underlying issues. Some common warning signs include:

Disrespectful Communication

- **Name-calling or Insults:** Using derogatory language during arguments signals a lack of respect.
- **Dismissive Behaviour:** Ignoring or belittling a partner's feelings or opinions can erode trust.

Control Issues

- **Decision-Making Dominance:** If one partner consistently makes decisions without consulting the other, it may indicate control rather than mutual respect.
- **Isolation from Friends/Family:** Attempts to limit contact with loved ones can signify manipulative behaviour.

Lack of Support

- **Neglecting Emotional Needs:** A partner who fails to support their spouse during challenging times may not value their emotional well-being.

- **Undermining Achievements:** Dismissing or downplaying accomplishments can reflect jealousy or insecurity rather than support.

Inconsistent Behaviour

- **Hot-and-Cold Dynamics:** Fluctuating between affection and withdrawal can create confusion about commitment levels.

- **Broken Promises:** Repeatedly failing to follow through on commitments undermines trust.

Recognising these red flags early on allows couples to address issues before they escalate into more significant problems.

In conclusion, mutual respect and love are foundational elements for a successful marriage, as highlighted in Ephesians 5:33. By understanding the importance of both components, assessing how they manifest in relationships, and being aware of potential red flags, couples can work towards building strong partnerships grounded in mutual admiration and affection.

CHAPTER 20: CONFLICT RESOLUTION SKILLS

The Necessity of Handling Conflicts Well (Proverbs 15:1)

Conflict is an inevitable part of any relationship, including marriages. Proverbs 15:1 states, "A gentle answer turns away wrath, but a harsh word stirs up anger." This verse underscores the importance of communication style in conflict resolution. Handling conflicts well is essential for maintaining healthy relationships and creating mutual respect between partners.

Importance of Effective Conflict Resolution

1. **Preservation of Relationships:** Effectively managing conflicts can prevent misunderstandings from escalating into larger issues that may threaten the stability of a relationship.

2. **Emotional Health:** Unresolved conflicts can lead to resentment and emotional distress. Addressing disagreements constructively promotes emotional well-being for both partners.

3. **Skill Development:** Learning to navigate conflicts enhances interpersonal skills such as empathy, active listening, and negotiation, which are valuable in all areas of life.

Strategies for Peaceful Resolution

To resolve conflicts peacefully, couples can employ several strategies:

1. Active Listening:

- Listening attentively to your partner's perspective without interrupting creates understanding and shows respect for their feelings.
- Reflecting back what you hear can clarify misunderstandings and demonstrate that you value their viewpoint.

2. Use "I" Statements:

- Framing concerns using "I" statements (e.g., "I feel upset when...") rather than accusatory "you" statements (e.g., "You always...") helps express feelings without placing blame.
- This approach reduces defensiveness and encourages open dialogue.

3. Stay Focused on the Issue:

- Address specific issues rather than bringing up past grievances or unrelated problems during a disagreement.
- Keeping discussions focused prevents escalation and allows for more effective problem-solving.

4. Seek Common Ground:

- Identifying shared goals or values can help partners find solutions that

satisfy both parties.
- Collaborating on compromises reinforces teamwork and strengthens the relationship.

5. Take Breaks When Needed:
- If emotions run high, taking a break to cool down can prevent hurtful comments or actions that may damage the relationship.
- Agreeing to revisit the discussion later allows both partners to approach the issue with a clearer mindset.

When Disagreements Become Toxic

While conflict is natural, some disagreements can become toxic if not managed properly:

1. Signs of Toxic Conflict:
- Frequent name-calling, insults or belittling remarks indicate a breakdown in respectful communication.
- Stonewalling or refusing to engage in discussions creates emotional distance and hinders resolution efforts.

2. Impact on Relationships:
- Toxic conflict can lead to long-term damage in relationships, resulting in decreased trust and intimacy.
- Partners may begin to feel emotionally unsafe, leading to withdrawal or avoidance behaviours.

3. Addressing Toxic Patterns:
- Recognising toxic patterns is the first step toward change. Couples should reflect on their interactions and identify harmful behaviours.
- Seeking professional help from counsellors or therapists can provide tools for breaking negative cycles and rebuilding healthy communication habits.

In conclusion, handling conflicts well is crucial for nurturing strong relationships, as emphasised by Proverbs 15:1. By employing strategies such as active listening, using "I" statements, staying focused on issues, seeking common ground, and knowing when to take breaks, couples can resolve disagreements peacefully. However, it is essential to recognise when conflicts become toxic and take proactive steps to address these patterns before they cause irreparable harm to the relationship.

CHAPTER 21 : COMMON RED FLAGS TO AVOID (1 CORINTHIANS 15:33)

In the context of relationships, red flags are warning signs that indicate potential problems or unhealthy dynamics. The biblical reference from 1 Corinthians 15:33 states, "Do not be misled: 'Bad company corrupts good character.'" This verse underscores the importance of being aware of the influences that others can have on our lives and relationships. Recognising common red flags can help individuals avoid entering or remaining in unhealthy relationships.

Emotional Manipulation

One significant red flag is emotional manipulation, where one partner uses guilt, fear, or obligation to control the other. This behaviour can manifest as constant criticism, gaslighting (making someone doubt their reality), or playing the victim to elicit sympathy. Such tactics undermine self-esteem and create an imbalanced power dynamic.

Lack of Respect

A lack of respect for boundaries is another critical warning sign. If a partner consistently disregards personal space, privacy, or individual needs, it indicates a fundamental disrespect that can lead to further issues down the line. Healthy relationships are built on mutual respect and understanding.

Excessive Jealousy

While some level of jealousy can be normal in relationships, excessive jealousy often points to insecurity and possessiveness. A partner who frequently questions your whereabouts, monitors your communications, or isolates you from friends and family may be exhibiting controlling behaviour that could escalate into more serious issues.

Inconsistent Communication

Communication is vital in any relationship. If one partner constantly avoids discussing important topics or becomes defensive when confronted about issues, it may signal deeper problems. Healthy communication involves openness and a willingness to engage in difficult conversations.

How to Walk Away from a Wrong Relationship

Recognising that a relationship is unhealthy is only the first step. Knowing how to walk away is equally important for personal well-being.

Acknowledge Your Feelings

The first step in walking away from a wrong relationship is acknowledging your feelings and recognising that you deserve better. Validating your emotions helps build the confidence needed to make difficult decisions.

Create a Support System

Before ending a relationship, it's beneficial to establish a support system consisting of friends or family members who understand your situation. They can provide encouragement and perspective during this challenging time.

Plan Your Exit Strategy

Leaving an unhealthy relationship requires careful planning. Consider logistics such as living arrangements, financial implications, and emotional readiness before making any final decisions. Having a clear plan can reduce anxiety about the transition.

Communicate Clearly

When you decide to end the relationship, communicate your decision clearly and respectfully. Avoid engaging in blame games; instead, focus on expressing your feelings honestly while maintaining dignity for both parties involved.

Trusting God's Guidance

In times of uncertainty regarding relationships, trusting God's guidance can provide clarity and peace:

Prayer for Wisdom

Engaging in prayer allows you to seek divine wisdom when facing tough decisions about relationships. Asking for guidance helps align your thoughts with spiritual values and provides comfort during transitions.

Seeking Counsel from Faith Leaders

Consulting with trusted faith leaders or mentors can offer valuable insights based on spiritual teachings. They can provide perspective on navigating relationships while adhering to one's beliefs.

Reflecting on Scripture

Turning to scripture for guidance can also be beneficial. Verses that emphasise love, respect, and healthy boundaries serve as reminders of what constitutes a healthy relationship according to faith principles.

In conclusion, recognising common red flags such as emotional manipulation, lack of respect, excessive jealousy, and inconsistent communication is crucial for maintaining healthy relationships. Walking away from wrong relationships involves acknowledging feelings, creating support systems, planning exits carefully, and communicating clearly while trusting God's guidance through prayer and reflection on scripture, which provides strength during these challenging times.

CHAPTER 22: COUNSELLING QUESTIONS FOR EACH SESSION IN THE PREMARITAL

Introduction: Premarital counselling is an essential step in preparing for a successful, Christ-centred marriage. Marriage is a covenant, not just between two people but with God, who is the ultimate foundation and guide for every relationship. As such, it is vital to approach this sacred union with prayer, intentionality, and a deep understanding of God's design for marriage.

The purpose of this chapter is to provide couples with thought-provoking questions and biblical principles that will guide them in building a strong, lasting, and loving marriage. This chapter is designed to help couples explore various aspects of their relationship – communication, faith, finances, intimacy, parenting, and spiritual growth – by reflecting on the challenges and blessings of life together through a biblical lens.

Throughout the book, we delve into practical and theological topics, addressing the importance of mutual respect, understanding, and clear communication. The Question & Answer format offers an opportunity for couples to openly discuss these issues before their wedding day, ensuring that both partners are united in their values, priorities, and vision for the future.

As couples engage with the questions and scriptures provided, they will find themselves better equipped to face the challenges that come with marriage, fully grounded in God's word and led by His Spirit. By exploring biblical principles and applying them to their relationship, couples can build a marriage that honours God and reflects His love to the world.

References:

Ephesians 5:31-33: "For this reason a man will leave his father and mother and be united to his wife, and the two will become one flesh. This is a profound mystery—but I am talking about Christ and the church."

Proverbs 3:5-6: "Trust in the Lord with all your heart and lean not on your own understanding; in all your ways submit to him, and he will make your paths straight."

1 Corinthians 13:4-7: "Love is patient, love is kind. It does not envy, it does not boast, and it is not proud. It does not dishonour others, it is not self-seeking, it is not easily angered, and it keeps no record of wrongs. Love does not delight in evil but rejoices with the truth. It always protects, always trusts, always hopes, always perseveres."

Session 1: Biblical Foundations of Marriage

Objective: To establish a strong biblical understanding of marriage.

Questions:
1. What does it mean for a marriage to be Christ-centred?
2. How do you view your role as a husband or wife according to the Scripture?
3. How will you nurture your spiritual relationship with your spouse?
4. In what ways can you serve each other in marriage?
5. How does the relationship between Christ and the Church inspire your view of marriage?

Session 2: Communication and Conflict Resolution

Objective: To teach healthy communication skills and biblical conflict resolution.

Questions:
1. How do you each express your emotions and needs in a relationship?
2. What are some areas where you struggle with communication?
3. When disagreements arise, how do you typically respond?
4. How will you ensure you listen to each other during conflicts?
5. What strategies can you use to resolve conflicts in a way that honours God?

Session 3: Finances and Stewardship

Objective: To establish financial principles that will guide the marriage.

Questions:
1. What are your individual views on money, saving, and spending?
2. How will you handle finances together as a married couple?
3. Are there any areas of debt or financial habits that need to be addressed

before marriage?
4. How do you plan to honour God with your finances (e.g., giving, tithing, saving)?
5. What financial goals do you want to achieve in your marriage, and how will you work towards them?

Session 4: Family Background and Expectations

Objective: To explore each person's family dynamics and expectations for the marriage.

Questions:

1. What family traditions are important to you, and how will you incorporate them into your marriage?
2. Are there any unresolved family issues that could affect your marriage?
3. How do you plan to manage relationships with your in-laws?
4. What does each of you expect from your spouse in terms of family involvement and boundaries?
5. How will you maintain a balance between your relationship with your spouse and your family?

Session 5: Intimacy and Emotional Connection

Objective: To foster emotional and physical intimacy in the marriage.

Questions:

1. How do you both express love and affection?
2. What emotional needs do you have in a marriage, and how will you meet each other's needs?
3. Are there any areas of physical intimacy that you need to address before marriage?
4. How do you plan to keep the emotional connection strong throughout the marriage?
5. How will you maintain purity and honor in your relationship before marriage?

Session 6: Shared Vision and Ministry

Objective: To align the couple's vision for their future together, including ministry.

Questions:

1. What is your individual vision for your life and how does it align with your spouse's vision?
2. How do you plan to serve God together as a couple?
3. What areas of ministry or service are you both passionate about?
4. How do you plan to balance your individual callings with your marriage responsibilities?
5. How will you pray and seek God's direction for your marriage and ministry?

Session 7: Identifying and Resolving Red Flags

Objective: To identify potential red flags and address unresolved issues.
Questions:

1. Are there any past unresolved conflicts or habits that could be problematic in marriage?
2. How do you each handle stress, disappointment, or emotional struggles?
3. Are there any behaviours or attitudes that are causing concern to you about your partner?
4. What steps can you take together to resolve any red flags before marriage?
5. How can you support each other in personal growth and overcoming challenges?

Session 8: Final Preparations and Wedding Planning

Objective: To prepare spiritually and emotionally for the wedding day and marriage.

Questions:

1. How are you preparing spiritually for the wedding and marriage?
2. What are your expectations for your wedding day, and how can you keep it in perspective?

3. How will you keep God at the centre of your marriage from the very beginning?
4. What are your final preparations for the transition into marriage?
5. How will you create and nurture a healthy marriage after the wedding day?

Expanded Counseling Questions for Each Session in the Premarital Counseling Plan

Session 1: Biblical Foundations of Marriage

Objective: To establish a strong biblical understanding of marriage. Expanded Questions:

1. What is your understanding of the concept of "one flesh" in marriage (Genesis 2:24)?
2. How do you believe your marriage will reflect Christ's love for the Church (Ephesians 5:25)?
3. What are some ways you plan to submit to one another out of reverence for Christ (Ephesians 5:21)?
4. In practical terms, how can you ensure that both of you grow spiritually together in marriage?
5. What specific prayers will you commit to praying together as a couple after marriage?
6. How will you handle disagreements or differences in faith (Romans 12:18)?

Session 2: Communication and Conflict Resolution

Objective: To teach healthy communication skills and biblical conflict resolution.

1. How do you both handle misunderstandings? What strategies do you have in place to avoid assumptions?
2. How will you express your love and disagreement in a way that nurtures the relationship (Ephesians 4:29)?
3. When conflict arises, what methods will you use to maintain peace and avoid escalation (Matthew 18:15-17)?
4. What role does forgiveness play in resolving conflicts, and how will you forgive each other as Christ forgave you (Colossians 3:13)?
5. Are there any habits or communication styles from your past relationships that need to be addressed?

6. How will you ensure that you both feel heard and valued during conflicts?

Session 3: Finances and Stewardship

Objective: To establish financial principles that will guide the marriage.
1. How do you plan to handle your finances: joint accounts or separate accounts?
2. How do you both feel about budgeting, saving, and spending?
3. What is your approach to tithing and giving, and how will you prioritise it in your marriage (Malachi 3:10)?
4. How do you plan to handle any debts or financial obligations before marriage?
5. Will you establish long-term financial goals as a couple (e.g., buying a house, saving for children's education)?
6. How do you plan to support each other's financial goals, even if one of you faces financial difficulty?
7. How will you handle differences in financial priorities or spending habits?

Session 4: Family Background and Expectations

Objective: To explore each person's family dynamics and expectations for the marriage.
1. What childhood values or traditions do you want to pass on to your new family?
2. How do you plan to build your own family traditions while respecting each other's families?
3. What are your expectations for how your spouse will interact with your family, and vice versa?
4. How will you manage any potential conflict or tension with in-laws, especially in matters of holidays, celebrations, or family events?
5. Are there any unresolved family issues, such as abuse, anger, or bitterness, that need to be addressed before marriage?
6. How can you both set healthy boundaries with your families to ensure your marriage remains the priority (Genesis 2:24)?

Session 5: Intimacy and Emotional Connection

Objective: To create emotional and physical intimacy in the marriage.

1. What does emotional intimacy look like for you, and how will you ensure it is nurtured daily in your marriage?
2. What role does physical intimacy play in marriage, and how will you keep that area pure and exciting (1 Corinthians 7:3-5)?
3. Are there any insecurities or past wounds related to intimacy that need to be healed?
4. How will you maintain a balance of affection, communication, and respect in your relationship?
5. What does "selflessness" in marriage look like to you, especially in terms of emotional and physical intimacy?
6. How will you ensure you have regular, quality time together to deepen your emotional connection?

Session 6: Shared Vision and Ministry

Objective: To align the couple's vision for their future together, including ministry.

1. How do you envision your roles in ministry, and how will you support each other in fulfilling these callings?
2. How do you see your marriage being a witness to others (Matthew 5:14-16)?
3. What specific ways will you both use your individual gifts in ministry while supporting your shared vision?
4. How will you handle disagreements or differing views on ministry involvement?
5. How do you plan to balance time between ministry commitments and personal time as a couple?
6. How will you remain spiritually strong together, even during busy or challenging ministry seasons?

Session 7: Identifying and Resolving Red Flags

Objective: To identify potential red flags and address unresolved issues.

1. Are there any behavioural patterns or emotional triggers that could be a potential issue in marriage?
2. What are your greatest fears about marriage, and how will you address them together?

3. How will you handle emotional outbursts or situations where one partner is more reactive than the other?
4. How do you plan to work through jealousy, insecurity, or feelings of inadequacy within the marriage?
5. Have you been fully transparent with each other about your past, habits, and struggles (Proverbs 28:13)?
6. What steps will you take if a red flag arises during the marriage?

Session 8: Final Preparations and Wedding Planning

Objective: To prepare spiritually and emotionally for the wedding day and marriage.
Expanded Questions:
1. How do you plan to ensure that your wedding is focused on glorifying God, not on worldly distractions (Colossians 3:23)?
2. How will you handle any pre-wedding stress or disagreements, ensuring the focus remains on your commitment to each other?
3. Are there any areas of wedding planning where one partner feels overwhelmed or underappreciated?
4. What steps will you take to spiritually prepare for the wedding day and beyond?
5. How can you continue to create a prayerful and intentional marriage from day one?
6. How will you set clear expectations for your first year of marriage, and what role will faith play in these preparations?

Expanded Counselling Questions

Session 1: Biblical Foundations of Marriage

Objective: To establish a strong biblical understanding of marriage.

Questions & Sample Answers:

1. What is your understanding of the concept of "one flesh" in marriage (Genesis 2:24)?

According to Genesis 2:24, the concept of "one flesh" in marriage signifies a deep, spiritual, physical, emotional, and covenantal union between a man and a woman, as instituted by God. The verse states, "Therefore a man shall leave his father and mother and be joined to his wife, and they shall become one flesh." This means that in marriage, two individuals are no longer separate but are united in purpose, love, and life. It implies complete intimacy, mutual commitment, shared responsibility, and an inseparable bond that reflects God's design for unity, harmony, and companionship in the marital relationship.

2. How do you believe your marriage will reflect Christ's love for the Church (Ephesians 5:25)?

I believe my marriage will reflect Christ's love for the Church by being rooted in selfless love, sacrifice, forgiveness, and unwavering commitment. Just as Christ gave Himself for the Church, I am committed to loving my spouse unconditionally, leading with humility, serving with joy, and building a relationship centred on grace, truth, and unity. Our marriage will strive to be a living testimony of God's covenant love, showing patience in trials, faithfulness in all seasons, and mutual respect that mirrors the relationship between Christ and His bride, the Church.

3. What are some ways you plan to submit to one another out of reverence for Christ (Ephesians 5:21)?

Some ways I plan to submit to one another out of reverence for Christ include practicing humility in our decisions, listening with empathy, valuing each other's opinions, and putting my spouse's needs above my own. I will strive to serve with love, communicate with grace, forgive quickly, and support my spouse's growth in Christ. By honouring each other's strengths and weaknesses and seeking God's will together, we create a relationship where mutual submission is not weakness but a reflection of our shared devotion to Christ.

4. In practical terms, how can you ensure that both of you grow spiritually together in marriage?

In practical terms, I can ensure that both of us grow spiritually together in marriage by making God the centre of our relationship through regular prayer, Bible study, and worship as a couple. We will set aside time to seek God's direction together, attend church and spiritual programs consistently, and hold each other accountable in our walk with Christ. I will encourage open conversations about faith, support my spouse's spiritual goals, and create an environment where we both feel safe to grow, learn, and serve God together in unity and love.

5. What specific prayers will you commit to praying together as a couple after marriage?

As a couple, I will commit to praying specific prayers that strengthen our spiritual bond and invite God's presence into every area of our lives. These include daily prayers for unity, wisdom, and guidance in our decisions; prayers for peace, love, and understanding in our home; prayers for each other's personal growth and purpose; and prayers for our future—our children, finances, health, and ministry. We will also pray for forgiveness, grace to overcome challenges, and strength to always honour God in our marriage. Through these prayers, we will continually invite Christ to be the foundation and centre of our union.

6. How will you handle disagreements or differences in faith (Romans 12:18)?

I will handle disagreements or differences in faith with humility, patience, and a commitment to love and unity. I will seek to listen respectfully, understand my spouse's perspective, and approach every difference with a heart willing to learn and grow. Instead of reacting emotionally, I will turn to prayer, the Word of God, and spiritual counsel when needed, trusting the Holy Spirit to bring clarity and peace. My goal will not be to win an argument but to preserve harmony and build each other up in Christ, knowing that our shared faith in Him is greater than any difference that may arise.

Session 2: Communication and Conflict Resolution questions:

1. How do you both handle misunderstandings? What strategies do you have in place to avoid assumptions?

I handle misunderstandings by choosing to pause, listen attentively, and seek clarity before reacting. To avoid assumptions, I commit to open and honest communication—asking questions when unclear and expressing my thoughts calmly. I also value checking in regularly with my spouse to ensure we're on the same page emotionally and spiritually.

2. How will you express your love and disagreement in a way that nurtures the relationship (Ephesians 4:29)?

I will express my love through kind, affirming words and consistent acts of care, while expressing disagreement respectfully and without bitterness. Guided by Ephesians 4:29, I will avoid harsh or destructive words, choosing instead to speak only what builds up and brings grace, even in difficult moments.

3. When conflict arises, what methods will you use to maintain peace and avoid escalation (Matthew 18:15-17)?

When conflict arises, I will first address the issue privately and gently with my spouse, following Matthew 18:15. If needed, I will seek counsel from a trusted spiritual mentor or church leader. I will remain prayerful, patient, and focused on resolving the issue, not attacking the person, to maintain peace and protect our bond.

4. What role does forgiveness play in resolving conflicts, and how will you forgive each other as Christ forgave you (Colossians 3:13)?

Forgiveness is essential to resolving conflict, as it allows healing and prevents bitterness. I will choose to forgive quickly and sincerely, just as Christ forgave me—without holding grudges or bringing up past wrongs. I will also ask for forgiveness when I'm wrong, creating a culture of grace and restoration in our marriage.

5. Are there any habits or communication styles from your past relationships that need to be addressed?

Yes, I recognise that in the past, I sometimes avoided confrontation, which led to unresolved tension. I am committed to breaking that pattern by facing issues with honesty, speaking up with love, and addressing matters early instead of letting them grow. I'm also learning to communicate more clearly rather than expecting my spouse to read my mind.

6. How will you ensure that you both feel heard and valued during conflicts?

I will ensure we both feel heard by actively listening without interrupting, affirming my spouse's feelings, and validating their concerns. I'll avoid dismissive language, be mindful of my tone, and create a safe space for open dialogue. I will also ask for feedback on how I can improve and make adjustments where needed to show that I value my spouse's voice.

Session 3: Finances and Stewardship

Objective: To establish financial principles that will guide the marriage.

Questions & Sample Answers:

1. How do you plan to handle your finances: joint accounts or separate accounts?

I plan to handle our finances through a joint account to promote transparency, trust, and unity. However, I'm also open to having individual accounts for personal needs, as long as we both agree and maintain open communication about our finances.

2. How do you both feel about budgeting, saving, and spending?

I believe in intentional budgeting, disciplined saving, and responsible spending. I value planning ahead and avoiding impulsive purchases. Together, we will create a realistic budget that reflects our goals and priorities, ensuring that we are faithful stewards of what God entrusts to us.

3. What is your approach to tithing and giving, and how will you prioritise it in your marriage (Malachi 3:10)?

My approach to tithing and giving is to honour God first with our income, in obedience to Malachi 3:10. We will prioritise tithing as a non-negotiable part of our financial plan and also commit to generous giving—supporting our church, missions, and those in need—as an expression of gratitude and faith.

4. How do you plan to handle any debts or financial obligations before marriage?

I plan to be open and honest about any existing debts or obligations and work with my spouse to create a clear repayment plan. Transparency and unity will guide us as we make wise decisions to reduce debt and avoid unnecessary financial burdens.

5. Will you establish long-term financial goals as a couple (e.g., buying a house, saving for children's education)?

Yes, I believe in setting long-term financial goals together, such as purchasing a home, building an emergency fund, investing wisely, and saving for our children's education. These goals will give our marriage direction and help us build a stable future together.

6. How do you plan to support each other's financial goals, even if one of you faces financial difficulty?

I plan to support my spouse's financial goals with understanding, encouragement, and teamwork. If one of us faces financial difficulty, we will stand together, reassess our plans, and adjust where necessary, never allowing shame or blame to divide us. Our unity, prayer, and shared faith in God's provision will keep us strong.

Session 4: Family Background and Expectations

Objective: To explore each person's family dynamics and expectations for the marriage.

Questions & Sample Answers:

1. What family values or customs from your childhood are important to you, and how will you incorporate them into your new family?

The family values from my childhood that I hold dear include mutual respect, strong prayer life, hard work, and honoring elders. I plan to incorporate these into our home by creating a culture of love, spiritual devotion, open communication, and hospitality.

2. How do you plan to build your own family traditions while respecting each other's families?

I plan to build our own family traditions—such as weekly devotionals, annual retreats, or special celebration rituals—while still respecting and including meaningful customs from each of our families. Our home will reflect a blend of both backgrounds under one God-centered identity.

3. What are your expectations for how your spouse will interact with your family, and vice versa?

I expect my spouse to treat my family with love, respect, and kindness, just as I will do with theirs. I also expect mutual boundaries that protect the sanctity of our marriage while still honoring our families.

4. How will you manage any potential conflict or tension with in-laws, especially in matters of holidays, celebrations, or family events?

If any conflict or tension arises with in-laws, especially during holidays or family events, I will ensure we approach it with prayer, unity, and maturity. We will communicate our decisions lovingly but firmly and stand together as one.

5. Are there any unresolved family issues, such as abuse, anger, or bitterness, that need to be addressed before marriage?

If there are any unresolved family issues like past abuse, anger, or bitterness, I am committed to addressing them through counseling, prayer, and healing before marriage so they don't become a burden in our home.

6. How can you both set healthy boundaries with your families to ensure your marriage remains the priority (Genesis 2:24)?

To set healthy boundaries, I will uphold Genesis 2:24—"a man shall leave his father and mother..."—by making our marriage the first priority. While we will honour our families, decisions affecting our home will always be made between us in agreement.

Session 5: Intimacy and Emotional Connection

Objective: To foster emotional and physical intimacy in the marriage.

Questions & Sample Answers:

1. What does emotional intimacy look like for you, and how will you ensure it is nurtured daily in your marriage?

Emotional intimacy for me means being deeply connected through vulnerability, trust, communication, and prayer. I will nurture it daily by being emotionally present, actively listening, and creating a safe space for my spouse to share freely.

2. What role does physical intimacy play in marriage, and how will you keep that area pure and exciting (1 Corinthians 7:3-5)?

Physical intimacy is a sacred part of marriage and a gift from God. I will keep it pure and exciting by being intentional, respectful, and attentive to my spouse's needs—remaining faithful to 1 Corinthians 7:3-5, where both partners serve one another in love.

3. Are there any insecurities or past wounds related to intimacy that need to be healed?

If there are any insecurities or past wounds related to intimacy, I will face them honestly—with God, with my spouse, and through necessary healing and counsel. I believe that nothing is too broken for God to restore.

4. How will you maintain a balance of affection, communication, and respect in your relationship?

I will maintain a balance of affection, communication, and respect by staying emotionally connected, affirming my spouse daily, and never allowing routine to replace intentional care. Respect will always be foundational, even during disagreements.

5. What does 'selflessness' in marriage look like to you, especially in terms of emotional and physical intimacy?

Selflessness in marriage, especially in intimacy, means putting my spouse's needs above my own, being sensitive to their emotions, and sacrificing personal comfort for our mutual fulfilment—always acting in love and without selfish motives.

6. How will you ensure you have regular, quality time together to deepen your emotional connection?

I will ensure we have regular quality time by protecting our schedules, going on intentional dates, praying together, and checking in emotionally—even amidst busyness—to ensure our bond grows stronger daily.

Session 6: Shared Vision and Ministry

Objective: To align the couple's vision for their future together, including ministry.

Questions & Sample Answers:

1. How do you see your ministry roles, and how will you help each other fulfil them?

I envision us walking in unity in ministry, with each of us playing a unique role according to our gifts. I will support my spouse's calling by encouraging, praying, and helping them thrive in what God has placed in their hands.

2. How do you see your marriage being a witness to others (Matthew 5:14-16)?

Our marriage will be a witness by the way we love, serve, and forgive one another—reflecting Christ's light (Matthew 5:14-16). We will be a testimony of what it means to build a Christ-centered home in a broken world.

3. What specific ways will you both use your individual gifts in ministry while supporting your shared vision?

\ We will each use our individual gifts—teaching, hospitality, leadership, music, or counselling—while staying committed to our shared vision. We will align our strengths to complement each other and advance God's kingdom together.

4. How will you handle disagreements or differing views on ministry involvement?

When disagreements arise in ministry, I will approach them with humility and open dialogue. We will pray together and submit our differences to God's wisdom, always prioritizing unity over personal preference.

5. How do you plan to balance time between ministry commitments and personal time as a couple?

To balance ministry and personal time, we will set clear boundaries—scheduling time for rest, family, and personal bonding. Ministry will not come at the cost of our marriage; rather, our home will be the first place of ministry.

6. How will you remain spiritually strong together, even during busy or challenging ministry seasons?

We will remain spiritually strong by staying rooted in the Word, praying daily together, attending retreats, and having spiritual mentors who keep us accountable. Even in busy seasons, we will make our relationship with God and each other non-negotiable

Session 7: Identifying and Resolving Red Flags

Objective: To identify potential red flags and address unresolved issues.

Questions & Sample Answers:

1. Are there any behavioural patterns or emotional triggers that could be a potential issue in marriage?

2. What are your greatest fears about marriage, and how will you address them together?

3. How will you handle emotional outbursts or situations where one partner is more reactive than the other?

4. How do you plan to work through jealousy, insecurity, or feelings of inadequacy within the marriage?

5. Have you been fully transparent with each other about your past, habits, and struggles (Proverbs 28:13)?

6. What steps will you take if a red flag arises during the marriage?

Session 8: Final Preparations and Wedding Planning

Objective: To prepare spiritually and emotionally for the wedding day and marriage.

Questions & Sample Answers:

1. How do you plan to ensure that your wedding is focused on glorifying God, not on worldly distractions (Colossians 3:23)?

2. How will you handle any pre-wedding stress or disagreements, ensuring the focus remains on your commitment to each other?

3. Are there any areas of your wedding planning where one partner feels overwhelmed or underappreciated?

4. What steps will you take to spiritually prepare for the wedding day and beyond?

5. How can you continue to create a prayerful and intentional marriage from day one?

6. How will you set clear expectations for your first year of marriage, and what role will faith play in these preparations?

Session 9: Financial Stewardship and Money Management

Objective: To help couples align their financial goals and values.

Questions & Sample Answers:

1. How do you view money and wealth, and how will you ensure it doesn't become a source of division in your marriage (Matthew 6:24)?

2. How do you plan to manage finances as a couple (Proverbs 21:20)?

3. What steps will you take to stay financially transparent with one another, especially when it comes to debt or financial struggles?

4. What is your plan for saving, investing, and planning for future needs (Proverbs 6:6-8)?

5. How will you handle differences in spending habits or financial priorities?

6. How will you give to the Lord and to others in need as part of your financial stewardship (2 Corinthians 9:7)?

Session 10: Long-Term Growth and Commitment

Objective: To establish a foundation for lifelong growth and commitment in marriage.

Questions & Sample Answers:

1. What does lifelong commitment mean to you, and how will you continue to grow together as a couple (Ephesians 5:31)?

2. How will you maintain a strong spiritual connection and continue to seek God's will for your marriage?

3. How will you continue to support each other's individual goals and dreams while growing together as a team (Philippians 2:4)?

4. What steps will you take to protect your marriage from external pressures or challenges (Matthew 19:6)?

5. How will you handle long-term changes or transitions in your lives, such as career changes, moving, or children (Romans 8:28)?

6. What legacy do you hope to leave as a couple, both in your family and in your community (Proverbs 13:22)?

Session 11: Handling Challenges and Building Resilience

Objective: To help couples prepare for challenges and develop resilience in their marriage.

Questions & Sample Answers:

1. What challenges do you anticipate facing in your marriage, and how do you plan to face them together (James 1:2-4)?

2. How will you handle conflicts that may arise in your marriage, and what steps will you take to resolve them peacefully (Ephesians 4:26)?

3. How will you build resilience as a couple when life becomes difficult (Romans 5:3-5)?

4. What role will forgiveness play in your marriage, and how will you ensure that bitterness does not take root (Colossians 3:13)?

5. How will you encourage each other to stay resilient and faithful, even when facing personal struggles or challenges (Hebrews 10:24-25)?

6. How will you celebrate victories and milestones together, ensuring that you remain grateful and grounded in your faith (1 Thessalonians 5:16-18)?

Session 12: Communication Skills and Conflict Resolution

Objective: To build strong communication skills and effective conflict resolution strategies.

Questions & Sample Answers:

1. What does healthy communication look like to you, and how will you ensure it remains a priority in your marriage (James 1:19)?

2. How will you handle miscommunication or misunderstandings in your relationship (Proverbs 18:13)?

3. What methods will you use to de-escalate arguments and prevent them from spiraling into conflict (Proverbs 15:1)?

4. How will you ensure that you both feel heard and understood in every conversation (Philippians 2:4)?

5. What role does patience play in communication, and how will you cultivate it (Colossians 3:12)?

6. What steps will you take to ensure that conflict resolution is done in a way that strengthens your marriage, rather than creating distance (Matthew 18:15)?

Session 13: Roles and Responsibilities in Marriage

Objective: To define roles and responsibilities in marriage, ensuring mutual support and teamwork.

Questions & Sample Answers

1. What are your expectations for your role in the marriage, and how will you ensure you fulfill them (Ephesians 5:22-33)?

2. How will you balance the division of household responsibilities and ensure that both partners are equally involved (1 Corinthians 12:25)?

3. What role do you see for each partner in raising children, should God bless you with them, and how will you support each other in this area (Proverbs 22:6)?

4. How will you ensure that both of you feel valued in your respective roles, and how will you communicate your needs (Romans 12:10)?

5. How will you encourage growth and development in your roles, both individually and as a couple (Galatians 6:9)?

6. How will you navigate situations where you feel one partner is overwhelmed or not fulfilling their role (1 Thessalonians 5:11)?

Session 14: Spiritual Growth and Prayer Life Together

Objective: To build a strong spiritual foundation by growing in prayer, Bible study, and serving together.

Questions & Sample Answers:

1. What does a thriving spiritual life look like for you as a couple (Matthew 18:20)?

2. How will you prioritise your personal relationship with God while nurturing your marriage (Matthew 6:33)?

3. What steps will you take to serve God together, whether in ministry or everyday life (1 Peter 4:10)?

4. How will you handle spiritual differences or disagreements, and how will you maintain unity in your faith (Romans 15:5-6)?

5. What role will fasting, prayer, and worship play in your marriage, especially in times of difficulty (Isaiah 58:6)?

6. How will you make sure to keep God at the center of your relationship through the years (Proverbs 3:5-6)?

Session 15: Establishing Traditions and Building a Legacy

Objective: To create meaningful traditions and leave a legacy of faith and love for future generations.

Questions & Sample Answers:

1. What traditions do you hope to establish in your marriage, and how will they reflect your values and faith (Deuteronomy 6:6-7)?

2. How will you encourage future generations to follow Christ and build upon the legacy you create (Proverbs 22:6)?

3. How will you handle passing on family values, faith, and lessons learned to your children or those who come after you (2 Timothy 2:2)?

4. What role do you see your marriage playing in the wider community, and how will you influence others with your example (Matthew 5:16)?

Session 16: Managing Finances Together

Objective: To build a strong financial partnership based on biblical principles.

Questions & Sample Answers:

1. How will you manage your finances together, and what is your plan for budgeting (Proverbs 21:5)?

2. How will you handle debt and financial obligations as a couple (Romans 13:8)?
3. What will your approach be to saving for future needs such as housing, retirement, and emergencies (Proverbs 6:6-8)?

4. How will you ensure that both partners are involved in financial decisions and that there's transparency (Ephesians 5:21)?

5. How will you handle differences in financial habits or views, and what will you do if conflicts arise (1 Timothy 6:10)?

6. What role will giving and generosity play in your financial partnership (Luke 6:38)?

Session 17: Intimacy and Physical Boundaries

Objective: To establish healthy boundaries and mutual understanding regarding intimacy in marriage.

Questions & Sample Answers:

1. What does healthy intimacy mean to you in a marriage, and how will you prioritise it (1 Corinthians 7:3-5)?

2. How will you establish physical boundaries before marriage to honour God and each other (1 Thessalonians 4:3-5)?

3. What steps will you take to ensure that intimacy in marriage is not just physical but also emotional and spiritual (Ephesians 5:31)?

4. How will you communicate about intimacy and your physical needs throughout your marriage (Proverbs 5:18-19)?

5. What role will prayer and God's guidance play in developing a healthy and God-honouring intimate life (Hebrews 13:4)?

Session 18: Handling Change and Transition in Marriage

Objective: To prepare for changes and transitions that will naturally occur in marriage.

Questions & Sample Answers:

1. How will you handle major life transitions, such as moving, career changes, or changes in health (Ecclesiastes 3:1)?

2. What steps will you take to maintain your relationship when faced with challenges such as job loss, health issues, or relocation (Isaiah 41:10)?

3. How will you ensure your marriage grows stronger during difficult or transitional times (Romans 5:3-5)?

4. How will you celebrate victories and milestones together, ensuring that both of you feel honoured and valued (Psalm 126:3)?

5. How will you prepare for the changes that come with aging and long-term commitment (Proverbs 16:9)?

Session 19: Long-Term Vision and Legacy Planning

Objective: To create a vision for the future of your marriage and family, with a focus on leaving a lasting legacy.

Questions & Sample Answers:

1. What long-term vision do you have for your marriage, and how will you build towards it (Habakkuk 2:2-3)?

2. How will you create a legacy of faith, love, and service for your children and future generations (2 Timothy 1:5)?

3. What steps will you take to ensure that your marriage continues to thrive and inspire others as the years go on (Proverbs 16:31)?

Session 20: Trust and Transparency in Marriage

Objective: To build a foundation of trust and openness, ensuring that both partners feel secure and valued in the relationship.

Questions & Sample Answers:

1. How will you build and maintain trust in your marriage (Proverbs 3:5-6)?

2. How will you handle situations where trust has been broken (Ephesians 4:32)?

3. What does full transparency look like in your relationship (1 John 1:7)?

4. How will you ensure your actions and words align with your commitment to trust and transparency (Matthew 5:37)?

Session 21: Self-Care and Personal Growth in Marriage

Objective: To encourage individual growth and self-care that will benefit both partners in the relationship.

Questions & Sample Answers:

1. How will you prioritise self-care while ensuring it enhances your marriage (1 Corinthians 6:19-20)?

2. How will you encourage each other's personal growth and individual passions (Ecclesiastes 4:9-10)?

3. How will you handle times when one partner feels overwhelmed or unfulfilled (Matthew 11:28-30)?

4. What role does prayer and spiritual growth play in personal development within marriage (James 1:5)?

Session 22: Forgiveness and Conflict Resolution

Objective: To establish a biblical framework for resolving conflicts with grace, understanding, and forgiveness.

Questions & Sample Answers:

1. How will you handle conflicts and disagreements in your marriage (James 1:19)?

2. What role does forgiveness play in resolving conflicts (Ephesians 4:32)?

3. How will you deal with recurring issues or misunderstandings (Philippians 4:6-7)?

4. How will you ensure that conflicts don't damage the emotional connection in your marriage (Proverbs 15:1)?

Session 23: The Role of Extended Family and Community

Objective: To set healthy boundaries and maintain a balanced relationship with extended family and the wider community.

Questions & Sample Answers:

1. How will you balance your marriage with the demands of extended family relationships (Genesis 2:24)?

2. How will you support each other in maintaining good relationships with your families (Romans 12:18)?

3. What role does community play in your marriage, and how will you build strong friendships with others (Hebrews 10:24-25)?

4. How will you maintain unity when family members or friends offer unsolicited advice (Proverbs 19:20)?

Session 24: Celebrating Your Marriage and Relationship with God

Objective: To emphasise the importance of regularly celebrating marriage and keeping God at the center of the relationship.

Questions & Sample Answers:

1. How will you celebrate milestones in your marriage, such as anniversaries or achievements (Psalm 126:3)?

2. How will you continue to build your relationship with God as a couple (Matthew 18:20)?

3. How will you continue to grow in love and appreciation for one another over the years (1 Corinthians 13:4-7)?

Session 25: Financial Stewardship and Partnership

Objective: To establish biblical principles for managing finances as a couple and ensuring that financial decisions align with God's will.

Questions & Sample Answers:

1. How will you approach financial decisions as a team (Proverbs 21:5)?

2. How will you manage debt and savings together (Luke 14:28)?

3. What are your views on tithing and giving as a couple (Malachi 3:10)?

4. How will you support each other in financial challenges (Philippians 4:19)?

Session 26: Sexual Intimacy and Purity in Marriage

Objective: To promote a healthy understanding of sexual intimacy within marriage, rooted in biblical principles and mutual respect.

Questions & Sample Answers:

1. How will you cultivate a strong and intimate sexual relationship (1 Corinthians 7:3-5)?

2. What role does purity play in your marriage (Hebrews 13:4)?

3. How will you address differences in sexual desires or preferences (Song of Solomon 4:9-10)?

4. How will you seek healing if there are past issues related to sexuality (2 Corinthians 5:17)?

Session 27: Parenting and Raising Children

Objective: To prepare couples for parenting, emphasising the biblical approach to raising children in a Christ-centred home.

Questions & Sample Answers:

1. What are your shared views on parenting, and how will you raise your children (Proverbs 22:6)?

2. How will you address differences in parenting styles (Ephesians 6:4)?

3. How will you balance time spent with your children and your marriage (Ecclesiastes 3:1-8)?

4. What role will discipline play in your parenting approach (Proverbs 13:24)?

Session 28: Spiritual Leadership and Serving Together

Objective: To explore how both partners can actively engage in spiritual leadership within the marriage and serve God together in ministry.

Questions & Sample Answers:

1. How will you serve God together as a couple (Colossians 3:17)?

2. How will you encourage spiritual leadership in your marriage (1 Corinthians 11:3)?

3. What is your approach to ministering to others as a couple (Matthew 25:35-40)?

4. How will you prioritise your personal and collective spiritual growth? (Psalm 119:11).

Session 29: Patience, Long-Suffering, and Endurance
Objective: To cultivate a heart of patience and endurance in marriage, especially during challenging times.

Questions & Sample Answers:

1. How will you cultivate patience in your relationship (James 5:7-8)?

2. How will you support each other in enduring through difficult times (Romans 12:12)?

3. How will you remain steadfast when your commitment is tested (Galatians 6:9)?

4. How will you celebrate endurance and growth in your marriage (Romans 5:3-5)?

Conclusion:

Marriage is a lifelong journey, and the foundation of any successful marriage is rooted in the faith, love, and grace of God. This Q&A for Premarital Counselling has been designed to help couples embark on this journey with clarity and purpose. The questions, paired with biblical principles, guide couples to examine their readiness for marriage, challenge them to deepen their understanding of each other, and encourage them to build a relationship grounded in Christ.

As you move forward in your marriage, remember that premarital counselling is not just a one-time event but a continual process of growth. The questions in this book are a starting point for deeper discussions, and the principles laid out throughout these pages should be revisited regularly throughout the course of your marriage. Communication, trust, and a shared commitment to God will be the cornerstones of your relationship, ensuring that it stands firm, even in the face of challenges.

Let this counselling guide serve as a reminder that marriage is a sacred covenant. One that requires not just love but commitment, respect, and a continuous pursuit of God's will. By maintaining an open heart, a willingness to grow together, and a dependence on God's grace, you will be well-prepared to build a marriage that honours Him.

As you begin this new chapter, may you experience the fullness of God's blessings in your relationship, reflecting His love in everything you do. Remember, a Christ-centred marriage is not only a source of joy and fulfilment but also a powerful testimony to the world of God's grace and faithfulness.

Bible Quotes

1 John 4:19 – "We love because he first loved us."

Romans 12:10 – "Be devoted to one another in love. Honor one another above yourselves."

Hebrews 13:4 – "Let marriage be held in honour among all, and let the marriage bed be undefiled; for God will judge the sexually immoral and adulterous."

With God at the centre, may your marriage be a beautiful reflection of His divine love.

REFLECTIVE NOTE FROM THE AUTHOR

Choosing a life partner is one of the most important decisions you will ever make; second only to your decision to follow Christ. Marriage can either build you or break you, depending on who you say "yes" to.

This book is written not to discourage you from marrying, but to prepare you for it. Many marriages suffer because people focus more on the wedding day than on what comes after it. But God wants us to go into marriage prepared; mentally, emotionally, spiritually, and practically.

My prayer is that you will read this book with a willing heart, apply its truths, and allow God to lead you to the right person at the right time for the right purpose. Remember: It is better to wait long than to marry wrong.

Pastor Chika Innocent Ugo

Healed By His Stripes Church International

Pastor Innocent Ugo

REFERENCES

DeLashmutt, G. (2015). Loving God's Way.

Fraley, B. and Christian Life Outreach (2007). Salt & light : fulfilling God's mission for America in these last days. Scottsdale, Ariz.: Christian Life Outreach.

Holy Bible (NIV). (2008). [S.l.]: Zondervan.

Joshua Jarvis. (2020). Why The Marriage Covenant Is So Important | Joshua Jarvis. [online] Available at: https://jrjarvis.com/why-the-marriage-covenant-is-so-important/ [Accessed 17 Mar. 2025].

Putman, J. (2025). Real-Life Discipleship. NavPress.

Rensburg, van (2024). God's Love Deal With Us. RWG Publishing.

Sproul, R.C. (2019). What Is Repentance? Reformation Trust Publishing.

The Rebel Christian. (2022). Christian Marriage: What is a Marital Covenant? [online] Available at: https://www.therebelchristian.com/blog/christian-marriage-what-is-a-marital-covenant4152022.

Walsh, S. (2021). Holding on When You Want to Let Go : Clinging to Hope When Life Is Falling Apart. [United States]: Baker Publishing Group.

www.preceptaustin.org. (n.d.). The Covenant of Marriage | Precept Austin. [online] Available at: https://www.preceptaustin.org/the_covenant_of_marriage [Accessed 28 Oct. 2022].

www.preceptaustin.org. (n.d.). The Covenant of Marriage | Precept Austin. [online] Available at: https://www.preceptaustin.org/the_covenant_of_marriage [Accessed 28 Oct. 2022].

www.ingramcontent.com/pod-product-compliance
Lightning Source LLC
Chambersburg PA
CBHW060452080526
44584CB00015B/1415